10/19
921 Cur

D1314770

WOMEN IN
SCIENCE

Marie Curie
*Radioactivity Pioneer
and the First Woman to
Win a Nobel Prize*

Cavendish
Square
New York

Maggie May Ethridge

Published in 2017 by Cavendish Square Publishing, LLC
243 5th Avenue, Suite 136, New York, NY 10016

Library of Congress Cataloging-in-Publication Data

Names: Ethridge, Maggie May.
Title: Marie Curie : radioactivity pioneer and first woman to win a Nobel Prize / Maggie May Ethridge.
Description: New York : Cavendish Square Publishing, [2017] | Series: Women in science | Includes bibliographical references and index.
Identifiers: LCCN 2016023217 (print) | LCCN 2016024757 (ebook) |
ISBN 9781502623096 (library bound) | ISBN 9781502623102 (E-book)
Subjects: LCSH: Curie, Marie, 1867-1934. | Women chemists--Poland--Biography. |
Women chemists--France--Biography. | Nobel Prize winners--Biography.
Classification: LCC QD22.C8 E84 2017 (print) | LCC QD22.C8 (ebook) | DDC 540.92 [B] --dc23
LC record available at https://lccn.loc.gov/2016023217

Editorial Director: David McNamara
Editors: Leah Tallon/Kristen Susienka
Copy Editor: Rebecca Rohan
Associate Art Director: Amy Greenan
Designer: Alan Sliwinski
Production Assistant: Karol Szymczuk
Photo Research: J8 Media

CONTENTS

Marie Curie as a young girl in Poland

INTRODUCTION

THE LIFE OF MARIE SKLODOWSKI CURIE

Marie Sklodowski Curie is one of the most important scientists in human history. Born November 7, 1867 to a poor but loving Polish family, she brought a deep intellect and ethics of hard work to her time of higher learning at the Sorbonne in Paris, France. At the Sorbonne, she met her husband, Pierre Curie. The Curies eventually had two daughters, Irène and Ève. Pierre was an important scientist, and the two married and began working together on Marie's thesis. Her thesis was built on the work of Wilhelm Röntgen and Antoine Henri Becquerel, two physicists. Curie herself was a chemist and physicist.

In July 1898, the Curies announced to the Academy of Sciences the discovery of a new chemical element, polonium. At the end of the year, another paper was presented to the Academy, announcing the discovery of another element, called radium. The Curies and their colleague, Henri Becquerel, were awarded the Nobel Prize for Physics in 1903 for their research on the phenomenon of radiation. The Curies had discovered the source of radiation, and proven that it came from the atomic level, which completely changed the scientific understanding of the atom.

Pierre Curie's life ended in 1906 after he was tragically knocked down and killed by a horse-drawn carriage. Soon afterward, Marie Curie took over his post as professor of general physics in the Faculty of Science, as the first woman to teach at the Sorbonne. She ensured the creation of The Radium Institute, of which she was also appointed director of the Curie laboratory. The Curie Foundation was established in 1920 and was quickly recognized as a public interest institution the following year, becoming a model for cancer centers around the world. In 1970, The Radium Institute and the Curie Foundation merged to become Institut Curie, with three missions of research, teaching, and treating cancer.

In 1911, Curie received a second Nobel Prize in Chemistry for her discovery of the elements polonium and radium. The discovery of radium led to some of the most important treatments of cancer. Radium has the ability to kill cells, so it is used for targeted elimination of cancer cells. Radium is also used in dating techniques on ancient objects, rocks, and the age of our universe, as well as for molecular biology and modern genetics. Marie Curie was the first woman to win a Nobel Prize, and she remains the only woman to win the award in two different fields.

The Curies' research was a crucial step in the development of surgical X-rays. During World War I, Curie designed ambulances equipped with unique X-ray equipment. Curie herself drove these vehicles on the front lines. The International Red Cross assigned her as head of radiological service, and injured soldiers in battlefield tents were assisted by her "Little Curies," the portable X-ray machines she had invented. Curie held training courses for medical orderlies and doctors so they could quickly absorb the new techniques, and she taught these techniques at The Radium Institute after the war.

By the late 1920s, her health was beginning to deteriorate from exposure to radiation. She died on July 4, 1934 from aplastic anemia, a disease of the bone marrow. The Curies' eldest daughter, Irène, was also a scientist and winner of the Nobel Prize in Chemistry. Like her mother, she would also die from effects of radiation exposure.

Despite her success, Marie Curie repeatedly encountered opposition from French male scientists, and she did not acquire financial gains from her research and discoveries, in part because she and Pierre had declined to patent their discoveries. Curie never regretted her decision, saying that radium was an element, and as such, belonged to the people. She was clear that scientific research had value in its contributions to mankind, not in monetary benefits.

Pictured here as a young student, Marie Curie was well known for her prodigious memory.

THE EARLY DAYS OF MARIE CURIE

Marie Sklodowski was born November 7, 1867, in Warsaw, Congress Kingdom of Poland, in the Russian Empire. She was the youngest of five siblings: Zosia, Jozef, Bronya, and Hela. Marie Curie's parents, Wladyslaw and Bronislawa Sklodowski, were both educators; her father was the president of Lublin University, and her mother was the principal of a girl's boarding school.

POLITICS AND FAMILY IN POLAND

Poland had been overthrown by Catherine the Great in 1790, and with increasingly burdensome Russian authority over time, Poland had, by the time Marie Curie was a girl, come under the control of a Russian czar who was attempting to completely eradicate Polish history. Russian was the official language, and people were not allowed to read or write in the Polish language.

In Curie's childhood, her family had a series of traumatic events. Curie's father lost his respected position because he was caught by the head inspector teaching Polish to his students, and in 1876, when she was ten, her older sister Zosia became ill and died from the disease **typhus**. Two years later, Curie lost her mother, Bronislawa, to tuberculosis.

Typhus and tuberculosis devastated Warsaw during the late 1800s. Only one house in three had running water, and only one in fifteen houses had a form of sanitation. Many of the streets were unpaved roads that ran with open sewers; these living conditions were the perfect breeding ground for both diseases. The combined death rate from them at that time has been stated at around thirty-two thousand people—sadly, Marie Curie's beloved mother and sister among them.

Bronislawa was an important influence on Marie Curie, although typically the focus has been on the influence of her father, since he was a gifted mathematics and physics teacher. Curie's mother, though restrained by the **mores** of her time, was an intellectual, educated at the Freta Street School, the only private girl's school in Warsaw. After Bronislawa graduated, she stayed on as headmistress and raised her family in the school apartment, reserved for the headmistress and family. Marie Curie said later of her mother:

> **❝** *This catastrophe was the first great sorrow of my life and threw me into a profound depression. My mother had an exceptional personality. With all her intellectuality she had a big heart and a very high sense of duty. And, though possessing infinite indulgence and good nature, she still held in the family a remarkable moral authority.* **❞**

WORK, REBELLION, AND EDUCATION

Because her father, Wladyslaw, lost his savings through bad investments, Curie had to take work as a teacher to help support her family. She also **clandestinely** participated in the nationalist "free university"— which defied the controlling Russian government—and read in Polish to female workers. Private education was forbidden, and only Russian schools were allowed. This important work was a quiet form of nonviolent rebellion, called organic work, which is work for education and prosperity; in particular, it was work to educate the peasants. If Curie had been caught, this crime was punishable by exile in Siberia.

Marie and her siblings. Left to right: *Zosia, Hela, Marie, Joseph, and Bronya.*

This rebellion through education was a good training ground for young Marie Curie, who was rapidly becoming a well-educated and opinionated intellectual during a time and place that did not allow women to be any of those things. Curie was unknowingly preparing herself for adult life, in which she would repeatedly butt against closed doors in the scientific and intellectual community, doors that were closed specifically because she was a woman.

Curie was an exceptional student who excelled in physics, chemistry, math, biology, and music. She had an outstanding memory and used it to learn Polish, Russian, English, and French. She dreamed of becoming a university student, but this dream had to be delayed. Because women could not obtain higher education in Poland, Curie would have to travel in order to attend a university, and Wladyslaw, already putting his son through school, did not have the funds to assist a daughter.

A GOVERNESS'S JOB

Instead of relying on her father, she took a position as a governess for the purpose of financing her sister Bronya's medical studies in Paris, France, with the understanding that Bronya would, in turn, later help Marie get an education. The family that Curie worked for had an eldest son, Kazimierz, who was a student at Warsaw University and two years older than Curie. She and Kazimierz fell in love and desired to be married, but it was not to be. His well-off family did not approve of a relationship with a mere governess, and although their relationship persisted for some months, eventually they parted for good.

At the time of her homecoming to Warsaw, Curie's cousin, Jozef Buguski, also returned to Warsaw. He had been away in Russia studying to direct The Museum at the Ministry of Industry and Agriculture, and he began teaching Curie wet bench chemistry (named so because most the work is done with liquids). She performed her first experiments in the museum laboratory, discovering her passion and talent for scientific laboratory research.

After Curie's three fairly despondent years as a governess, her father obtained a position as the director of a reformatory and was able to assist his daughter Bronya himself. Finally, Curie was able to join her married sister in Paris.

Marie as a determined young college student, having just arrived at the Sorbonne in Paris

SORBONNE

Curie enrolled as a student of physics at the Sorbonne in Paris in early November 1891, as a twenty-four-year-old student in the faculty of the sciences. During her long years as a governess, she had followed her interest in mathematics and physics and studied on her own. She quickly realized yawning gaps in her learning compared to her French counterparts. She determinedly took to her studies with all the hard work and intellectual vigor that had been restrained during her years as a governess. She also struggled with the language. Although she had thought herself to be fluent in French, she found that listening to and comprehending native speakers was much more difficult.

Curie lived at first with her sister and her sister's husband, but the living conditions did not prove to be suitable for focused studying, so she moved into a small attic room closer to the university. This was a bold and unusual move, as during this time in France, proper ladies did not leave their homes unescorted, or walk through the streets of the Latin Quarter where she now abided. Even Curie's presence as a student at the university was unusual. She was one of only 210 female scholars, compared to the 9,000 men enrolled. Most of the women enrolled were, like Curie, foreign students. This was because girls' schooling in France did not provide the proper courses necessary to pass the **baccalaureate** exam required to attend university. French female students in Paris were outnumbered by their foreign counterparts.

At this time in France, some women were just beginning to attempt to engage in higher learning, a movement set in motion when in 1861, a young French woman passed her baccalaureate exam in Lyon. The theoretical right of access to higher education only began in 1880, and in Curie's time was still very much a shocking way of thinking. The Paris academic district, where Marie Curie lived and learned, was

GABRIEL LIPPMANN

 Gabriel Lippmann was an important influence on Marie Curie. A brilliant professor of physics at the Sorbonne, Lippmann did early studies in the field in which Pierre Curie had pioneered: electrical effects in crystals. Lippmann was Marie Curie's thesis advisor, and he let her use his laboratory for her thesis work. He also introduced Marie to Pierre, who was one of Lippmann's best students. Lippmann also gave Marie Curie her first job, in the form of a commission from the Society for the Encouragement of National Industry to do a study on the magnetic properties of various steels.

Gabriel Lippmann received the Nobel Prize in Physics in 1908 for producing the first color photographic plate. His search for a direct color-sensitive medium in photography resulted in important photographic advances. In 1891, Lippmann showcased an innovative color-photography process, later named the Lippmann process, that utilized the natural colors of light wavelengths instead of using dyes and pigments. Lippmann placed a reflecting coat of mercury behind the **emulsion** of a panchromatic plate. The ensuing reflection formed an unrealized image that altered in depth according to each ray's color. The development process then reproduced this image, and the result was startlingly accurate. This direct method of color photography was drawn out because of necessarily long exposure times, and it was not possible to make duplicates of the original. Probably because of this, the process never achieved popularity, but it was a crucial step in the development of color photography.

responsible for nearly half of all female enrollments, and the one with the most foreign women.

University schooling overtook her life, to the point where she was not eating enough and became ill. Her sister Bronya and Bronya's husband had to care for Curie until she was healthy again. This was, in part, caused by her small living allowance, which had to be distributed largely between tuition fees, food, and fuel (which could be costly) for warmth.

Curie was absorbed by the lectures of scientists Paul Appel, Edmond Bouty, and Gabriel Lippmann at the Sorbonne. She met well-known physicists Jean Perrin, Charles Maurain, and Aimé Cotton. She came in first in her master's degree physics course in 1893. Curie's in-depth physics research had led her to believe she must have just as firm a grasp on mathematics, in order to fully understand and utilize her physics knowledge. Lack of money almost stood in the way of obtaining her math degree, but a classmate at the Sorbonne had, unknown to Curie, put her name in for a scholarship. She was awarded the Alexandrovitch Scholarship for Polish students who desired to study abroad. The money she was given assisted her for one full year of schooling.

LOVE AND A LABORATORY

In 1894, Curie was actively seeking a research laboratory in order to work on her project: measuring the magnetic properties of various steel **alloys**. Through the suggestion of a friend, she visited Pierre Curie, the chief of the laboratory at the School of Physics and Chemistry at the University of Paris. He was a respected chemist involved in researching the physics of crystals. Pierre was instantly won over by the young scientist, and their courtship progressed from exchanging interesting scientific data to more personal letters. Pierre wrote to her that it would

In this wedding photo of Marie and Pierre Curie, Marie is wearing a practical gown that could be also used in the lab.

be wonderful "to spend life side by side, in the sway of our dreams: your patriotic dream, our humanitarian dream, and our scientific dream."

Marie and Pierre had much in common. Both came from very close, intellectual families that prized education and had strong patriotic tendencies. Both greatly valued literature as well as science, and both had put aside personal preferences in order to help support their families. They also had in common their lack of religion, devotion to scientific research, and love of travel.

Marie Curie was conflicted. Although she had strong feelings for Pierre, she was unsure about the prospect of living permanently in Paris, so far away from her remaining family in Poland. She had always intended to move back to Poland to be close to her beloved father. Eventually, Pierre asked Curie for her hand in marriage, and she accepted. They were married July 26, 1895 in the local town hall. The wedding was attended by Marie's father and her sister Hela, as well as her sister Bronya, Bronya's husband, and Pierre's family.

Marie and Pierre honeymooned on new bicycles through the Île-de-France. After returning to Paris, they began working side by side in Pierre's laboratory, the basis for most days of the rest of their marriage.

The great Eiffel Tower in Paris,
France, in the early 1900s

CHAPTER TWO

THE WORLD AS IT WAS DURING MARIE CURIE'S TIME

Paris is in northern France, at the center of the Île-de-France region, where Curie and Pierre happily biked during their honeymoon. The Seine, Oise, and Marne Rivers cross the Île-de-France. Île-de-France is also encircled with magnificent forests, including Rambouillet, Compiegne, and Fontainebleau. Fontainebleau in particular is famous for its startling beauty. The forests form a ring around the city known as "the lungs of Paris," as they filter the smoggy city air and provide oxygen. Curie and Pierre both loved the forests, and Curie actually stayed in a small forest town during a period of recovery from a lingering cough.

The area contained in the city limits is diminutive: no corner is farther than about 6 miles (10 kilometers) from the square in front of Notre Dame Cathedral. The cathedral sits in a depression in the ground, worn deep by the Seine. The Seine runs for 8 miles (13 km) through the middle of the city. The surrounding heights are considered the limits of the city proper.

BELLE EPOQUE

The *Belle Epoque,* translated as "beautiful age," is the French name for the period that loosely began at the end of the Franco-Prussian War (1871) and ended at the start of World War I (1914). This time period was so named due to increased standards of living and security for the upper and middle classes, whereas the lower classes did not equally benefit. The lower classes did benefit to some degree, but many urban dwellers remained in small living quarters, underpaid, and struggling with health issues.

It was just before the Belle Epoque in 1853 that Napoleon III appointed Baron Georges-Eugène Haussmann as prefect, and the beginning of Paris's transformation was at hand. Entire neighborhoods were demolished and redesigned to boast numerous wide boulevards, parks, squares, and quays that still exist today, right up next to office buildings and housing. The influx of people living in the countryside moving to the city doubled the population. Paris was truly transformed from a medieval city to a modern one. Additionally, the iron, chemical, and electricity industries grew, and in the early 1900s, there were 600 car manufacturers in France and 150 different makes of car. France was the world's largest car exporter. After the popularization of the telegraph and telephone, communications in France increased. Simultaneously, railways expanded exponentially. Agriculture was altered forever by artificial fertilizers and newly invented machines. The average French consumer was spending more, due to the mass production of goods as well as the rise in wages—up 50 percent for some.

A socialist party had struggled to coalesce in France, ultimately splitting into two very different parties in 1902: the Socialist Party of France, and the French Socialist Party. From 1899 to 1905, the "Bloc Republicain" provided France with relatively stable government. Curie was not politically active and largely remained focused on her family and research, although she deeply valued living in a free country and did speak out against the intellectuals who supported or encouraged Germany's plans for domination.

Curie's most political act was to accept membership in an arm of the League of Nations, called the International Committee on Intellectual Cooperation (ICIC). The ICIC, established in 1922 as a way for intellectuals of different nations isolated by war to be brought together, was first funded by France, and later by other governments as well. Curie persuaded Albert Einstein to join ICIC, too. Curie managed to utilize ICIC in order to assist a cause dear to her heart: the plight of poor students with potential to be important scientists, artists, writers, and so on, but who did not have the means to pursue their talents. During a committee meeting, Curie proposed that the group fund a summer vacation program for exceptional young scientists in the lower classes. Eventually, the program was funded.

Trade unions were legalized in 1884 and combined to form a national General Confederation of Labour in 1895. Its leaders favored sabotage, boycotts, and general strikes to move France toward a worker's state.

Bicycle use—Curie and Pierre's preferred form of transport—rose from 375,000 in 1898 to 3.5 million by 1914. Running water, gas, electricity, and functioning plumbing had been considered to be for the upper class only, and now they became available to the middle class and occasionally the lower classes. Sport, to play or to observe, became a larger national pastime.

The world-famous Eiffel Tower was completed in March 1889, for the 1889 Exposition Universelle, which was to celebrate the one-hundred-year anniversary of the French Revolution. It was meant to be temporary, but it remained the world's tallest building until 1930. Paris's

World's Fair was important to the economy, as it pushed enormous amounts of money into Parisian businesses and established the city as a tourist destination. The World's Fair of 1900 was also important to Pierre and Marie Curie, as they presented their eagerly anticipated paper at the International Congress of Physics: "The New Radioactive Substances and The Rays They Emit."

FRENCH DAILY LIFE

Sanitation in late nineteenth-century France was medieval, but slow change was coming. At the time, baths were taken only once a year, and there was no toilet paper; instead, a French person would use a small, folded cloth. Underclothing was seldom changed, while shirts that often doubled as nightshirts would be worn more than a week before being washed. At times, the collar and cuffs might be detached and cleaned on a daily basis. Shampoo was nonexistent, and hair was unwashed.

As French living became slightly more sanitary, and some new discoveries in the handling of disease came about, life expectancy increased. In the mid-eighteenth century, life expectancy was a mere twenty-five years; by the end of the century it was thirty years, and in 1810—partly due to the smallpox vaccination—it reached thirty-seven years. Life expectancy continued increasing during the nineteenth century, to forty-five years in 1900.

ANARCHY

When Alfred Nobel invented dynamite in 1867, he had no way of knowing that it would be used in deadly attacks in the name of **anarchy**. The aim of anarchy was to represent the highest ideals of the French Revolution, which were fairness, efficiency, and equality in the structure of society. Possibly the first self-proclaimed anarchist—and certainly one of the most important figures of **anarchy** at the turn of the century—was Frenchman Pierre-Joseph Proudhon, who famously asserted: "Whoever lays his hand on me to govern me is a usurper and tyrant, and I declare him my enemy." Proudon's central idea was "mutualism," an economic concept that aimed to move focus away from making money and pushed for banks with free credit and labor unions.

Between 1892 and 1894, Paris was held in fear by anarchists who blew up eleven bombs, using the most violent interpretation of the anarchist slogan, "Propaganda by Deed"—actions in place of words. Bombs erupted in the Chamber of Deputies, as well as restaurants, military barracks, and law offices. Less than a dozen people died in these anarchist attacks, but the city was in the grips of the fear of unstoppable and unpredictable violence that terrorism brings.

One of the most famous attacks was that of Emile Henry, a young, poor, Parisian intellectual. Henry entered a popular Parisian café, the Café Terminus on Gare Saint-Lazare, and with a homemade bomb, killed one and injured twenty more. Henry was caught and proclaimed no remorse, for he claimed "petty bourgeois with a steady salary in their pockets" were as much to blame for the inequality and suffering as government and society's elite. Henry was sentenced to death in 1894, a year in which Marie Curie was completely consumed in earning her physics degree and meeting Pierre Curie for the first time.

POSITIVISM

Positivism is a philosophical **ideology** that began with French philosopher Claude-Henri Saint-Simon (1760-1825), referring to a scientific approach to the world. Positivism offered an empirical as opposed to a theoretical approach to solving problems and crafting a superior society, using systems confined to the data of experience and excluding **metaphysical**, or abstract, speculations. Saint-Simon believed the implications of positivism could be utilized in social, political, educational, and even religious affairs, hoping to bring reform in each area.

Positivism's roots go even deeper. In the 1500s, Francis Bacon, philosopher and scientist, introduced a combination of induction and experiment as scientific method. This was a contrast from the scientific method used at the time, which was based on theory and deduction, not observation and experimentation and records. Modern naturalists believe that the world as it is can be explained through rigorous verification of the facts, and that if a theory cannot be verified, it cannot be claimed to be real. It was this scientific thinking that led to Claude-Henri Saint-Simon's theory, which then influenced Auguste Comte.

Auguste Comte was a student of Saint-Simon and a French philosopher who made positivism widely popular among the culture. Comte, widely regarded as the first true sociologist, put forth that societies progress from a theological stage (meaning a stage of much thinking and wondering and guessing) to a metaphysical one (meaning a stage of focusing on the philosophy of the meaning of being and knowing), then embracing a scientific stage created with the positivistic, scientific outlook and method. In Poland, positivism, as it was when Marie Curie was a young girl, had been embraced as a movement that included social and material reform and included women. Curie was magnetically drawn toward positivism, as she had lost her faith in an all-knowing, purposeful God after the untimely and heartbreaking deaths of her sister and still-young mother. The structure of positivism shows primarily in Marie Curie's legendary scientific rigor. Positivism rejects any beliefs that are not verified through scientific experimentation, and

Curie was obsessive on maintaining meticulous note-keeping, structure, and purity of her scientific process. Positivism fit with not only Curie's natural curiosity and inclination toward the sciences, but also with her desire to have the same opportunities as a young girl and woman in Poland as men did. She once wrote that she believed that positivist ideas were the best chance that Poland had for social progress. She felt the focus on individual improvements and responsibility had to come before broader issues could be resolved. Curie's entire life was a testament to her belief in the need for an individual to be responsible for themselves, down to her refusal to take a pension from France after the untimely death of her husband, Pierre. She maintained that since she was able to work, she would not feel right in taking money from the government.

Auguste Comte's **epistemological** argument, or argument about how human beings learn what we learn, remained close to the ideas of his naturalist predecessors, such as Francis Bacon, who believed that scientific knowledge about life comes from empirical observation. Comte also drew clear lines between empirical and normative knowledge. He proposed that knowledge not empirically founded was not information about the actual world, therefore falling outside the range of science.

Historically, positivism allows the scientist to choose from a certain scope of methods when investigating the actual, or "real," world. A positivist approach includes a hierarchy, or ranking, of methods in which experiments are considered the best option because of their ability to determine what the ultimate cause of a result is.

It is easy to see the appeal of positivism for Marie Curie. Following in her father's footsteps, she was already fascinated with physics and math. Positivism, with its focus on experiments as well as social justice through quantifiable measures, fit with Curie's growing belief that only what could be experimented with and proven was "real," as well as her desire for social reform, born through her own family's experiences as Polish citizens controlled by a Russian czar driven to extinguish Polish culture, as well as the systematic suppression of women in all areas of society outside the home.

THE FLOATING UNIVERSITY

Before leaving Poland for her schooling in Paris, Curie joined the "Floating University," an illegal night school where the students met each time at a different location, in order to better evade the czarist authorities. She was unable to attend university in her homeland, while her brother Joseph was enrolled in the medical school at the University of Warsaw. Students at the Floating University hoped their grassroots educational movement would be a part of a Polish liberation.

Actual professors did some of the instructing at the Floating University, but much was taught by whichever student was best informed on a subject, often in the form of a lecture. Pamphlets and articles were passed around in lieu of textbooks. At this time, there was a particular emphasis on the sciences, as new breakthroughs in learning were occurring around the world.

Curie said of her involvement with the Floating University:

❝ *It was one of those groups of Polish youths who believed that the hope of their country lay in a great effort to develop the intellectual and moral strength of the nation … we agreed among ourselves to give evening courses, each one teaching what he knew best.* **❞**

Charles Darwin, the great explorer and scientist who proposed the evolutionary theory of life

SCIENTIFIC BREAKTHROUGHS

One of those breakthroughs had been Charles Darwin's theory of evolution, which he presented in the famous 1859 book entitled *On the Origin of Species*. This important scientific script was immediately well received, though controversial. The first edition, published on November 24, 1859, sold out completely in one day; the book went through a total of six editions.

Darwin's theory of evolution is essentially the belief that all life has descended from a common ancestor, from plant to animals. Darwin's seed theory begins with the creation of life from nonlife; in other words, complex creatures evolve from more basic ancestors over time. Natural selection proposes that as random genetic mutations occur inside an organism's genetic code, beneficial mutations are preserved and passed on to the next generation because they aid survival. Over time, the accumulation of mutations results in an entirely different organism.

Darwin's ideas brought swift critique from religious leaders, as the theory was seen as going in the face of the belief behind many of the world's predominant religions, which is that man is a higher being who shares earth with many creatures, but was separately created from them. The English high-ranking Catholic official, Henry Cardinal Manning, condemned Darwin's views as "a brutal philosophy—to wit, there is no God, and the ape is our Adam."

One of the most respected religious leaders of nineteenth-century England, Samuel Wilberforce, the Anglican Archbishop of Oxford, disparaged natural selection for what he believed the theory lacked, in an 1860 meeting of the British Association for the Advancement of Science. Wilberforce reportedly asked biologist Thomas Henry Huxley if he was related to an ape on his grandmother's or grandfather's side. Huxley, a defender of evolutionary theory, earning him the nickname "Darwin's bulldog," reportedly answered that he would rather be the ancestor of a monkey than an advanced human being who used "knowledge and eloquence in misrepresenting those who are wearing out their lives in the search for truth."

Other scientific breakthroughs had come from Frenchman Louis Pasteur. Pasteur was a student at the Ecôle Normale in Paris; in 1843, he became a research chemist. In 1854, he became dean of the Faculty of Sciences at the University of Lille, and it was after this that he made his first, great scientific find: germs. After much public vilification and disbelief, he finally proved his germ theory beyond a shadow of a doubt. Next, Pasteur made the country of France happy when he found the amazing truth that heating wine to 55 degrees Celsius (131 degrees Fahrenheit) killed bacteria without ruining the taste of the wine. This process, called pasteurization, saved France's wine industry.

Pasteur resigned from the Ecôle Normale Superieure in 1876, becoming the appointed professor of chemistry at the Sorbonne—the same university that Marie Curie would attend years later. Pasteur discovered how to create a vaccine for chicken cholera in his lab. This discovery led to Pasteur's work in creating a successful vaccine for anthrax in sheep. Afterward, he turned his attention toward the dreaded and deadly disease of rabies.

Pasteur vaccinated Joseph Meister in 1885. Meister was an unfortunate nine-year-old boy who was attacked and bitten by a rabid dog. The vaccine worked very well, and Pasteur became famous. Pasteur's rabies vaccine saved hundreds of lives around the world, and his scientific breakthroughs on germs ushered in the era of preventive medicine. An international fundraiser was held to procure the funds to build the Pasteur Institute in Paris. The institute was inaugurated on November 14, 1888, and was built for the scientific research of infectious diseases in animal and plants.

By the time Curie was awarded her PhD from the Sorbonne in 1903, the Pasteur Institute of Paris was a beehive of scientific exploration and research. Scientists who researched at the institute were known as "Pastorians," following the scientific methods and ideology of their respected founder, Louis Pasteur. Pasteur's discoveries and research within the field of prevention and vaccination are credited for a sea change in the scientific approach to disease, as well as greatly reduced rates of illness and mortality around the turn of the century.

WOMEN'S RIGHTS IN THE MID TO EARLY 1900S

It was a thrilling time for a budding young scientist such as Marie Curie, absorbing lectures at the Floating University, and afterward studying at the Sorbonne before researching in the laboratory with her husband, Pierre Curie. However, despite the breakthroughs in public acceptance of scientific ideas and the scientific and medical communities themselves, this new expansion of thinking did not include women.

"Feminisme" in France

Women in the 1800s and early 1900s in France were denied the right to vote; forbidden from being a part of political clubs or going to meetings; excluded from candidacy, imprisoned; and legally, second-class citizens in almost every respect. It was not until 1881 that a French woman could open a savings account at a bank without her husband's direct approval.

Although the corset had begun its slow descent into oblivion elsewhere, it was still the dominant, expected fashion for French women. Corsets were redesigned to offer more freedom of movement, with the removal of tight-lacing and the S-line, and the addition of elastic inserts.

In the 1890s, there was a vigorous public debate in regards to women's rights. Hubertine Auclert was the founder of the French women's **suffrage** movement. She worked tirelessly for more than thirty years to win the vote for women through her suffrage league, a militant newspaper, and protests and boycotts which included violent demonstrations. In the 1890s, Auclert's term "feminisme," or feminism, became commonly used to describe the growing movement for women's rights. However, as male legislators refused to assist women in achieving their rights, women realized that the only way toward their goals—

French feminists agitate for change, holding and burning newspapers that read, "The Frenchwoman Must Vote."

including right to work and equal pay, and issues over parenthood and sexuality, among others—was to obtain political power. Unfortunately, it would not be until 1944 that women obtained the right to vote.

Women's Movement in the United States

In 1848, the first women's rights convention to discuss the condition of women in the United States was held in Seneca Falls, New York. Held over a period of two days, the convention allowed only women to speak on the first day and included men on the second. The convention's founders were Elizabeth Cady Stanton and Lucretia Mott, who had attended London's World Anti-Slavery convention and left angered at the exclusion of women. They determined the idea of the women's rights convention then and there.

Attended by a total of two hundred women and one hundred men, the convention was made powerful through the Declaration of Sentiments, Stanton's document that laid out the foundation of women's rights. At the end of the convention, sixty-eight women and thirty-two men signed the document.

After the 1866 American Anti-Slavery Society Meeting in Boston, suffragist Susan B. Anthony and abolitionist Lucy Stone devised the idea of an organization that joined the fight for rights for both women and black people: the American Equal Rights Association (AERA). Elizabeth Stanton and Frederick Douglass were cofounders. This organization only worked harmoniously for a few years, until the news of a coming Fifteenth Amendment that granted free men of color the right to vote. Many in the AERA were pleased with the amendment, considering it a move in the right direction, while others believed that leaving out the right for women to vote was unacceptable. Stanton and Anthony split from the AERA and formed the National Woman Suffrage Association, with the sole mission of achieving voting rights for women.

Suffragist Lucy Stone, meanwhile, created the American Woman Suffrage Association, which worked to secure women's rights through state legislation. Eventually, in 1890, the AWSA merged with the National Woman Suffrage Association, becoming the National American Woman Suffrage Association; this was the same year that the state of Wyoming entered the Union with women's suffrage.

Women's Suffrage in Great Britain

Great Britain's movement toward women's liberation truly stirred to life at the moment philosopher John Stuart Mill presented an act to Parliament, calling for inclusion of women's suffrage in the Reform Act of 1867. Also in 1867, Lydia Becker founded the first women's suffrage committee. Other such committees followed and in 1897, all the committees united as the National Union of Women's Suffrage Societies, choosing Millicent Garrett Fawcett as president. Fawcett set the tone for the group's more aggressive activities. Frustrated by the dominating social and political mores, some suffragettes became more militant.

Emmeline Pankhurst was the founder of the Women's Social and Political Union in 1903. Her followers, called "suffragettes," were vital and brave in the fight for women's rights. They publicly challenged politicians, participated in civil disobedience, and put themselves in the position to be arrested for causing riots. In 1913, Emily Davison of the Women's Social and Political Union died when she purposefully threw herself under the king's horse at the Epsom Derby in protest of the government's ongoing failure to grant women the right to vote. At the beginning of World War I, the advocates of women's suffrage stopped their activities in order to support the war effort. Women over the age of thirty received the right to vote in February 1918.

In general, the beginning of the twentieth century saw a new generation of suffragists who were tired of the movement's inactivity and inability to move the needle. Taking cues from the British women's movement, women in the US movement became more aggressive in their protest methods, using larger-scaled protests in more public venues, with a more militant approach. Many suffragists were arrested and endured being force-fed during their hunger strikes.

WOMEN IN SCIENCE

Women in the nineteenth century did not typically receive higher education. Before the early nineteenth century, women were generally prevented from accessing formal scientific training, so that only women with money could pursue scientific study. Women's colleges were originally begun in order to assist women in becoming better wives and mothers, but this crack in the dam released a steady, societal pressure for more opportunities for women to learn, brought on by women who pursued careers instead of only married life, women who taught at the colleges, and active feminists. Even as women began slowly attending these colleges, learning what was considered difficult—such as advanced mathematics, Greek, and Latin—the prevailing thought was these subjects were either too complex for women or, even worse, dangerous. It was argued that such learning would overeducate a woman and pull her from her societal calling as a wife and mother.

Elizabeth Blackwell was born in Britain and immigrated to the United States, becoming the first woman to earn a medical degree in the year 1849. However, some argue that James Barry might have actually been the first woman to obtain a degree. Barry was a British military surgeon who many historians believe may have been a woman masquerading as a man, and who, in 1812, was admitted as a doctor.

Sofya Vasilyevna Kovalevskaya was a more fitting cohort to Marie Curie, for her sharp scientific intellect, her interest in literature and writing, and her determination to achieve her goals in a male-dominated world. Kovalevskaya was born on January 15, 1850, in Moscow, Russia, and was a mathematician and writer. She was the first woman in Europe to obtain a doctorate in mathematics, the first to join the editorial board of a journal devoted to the sciences, and the first to be appointed professor of mathematics.

In 1868, Kovalevskaya agreed to a marriage of convenience with paleontologist Vladimir Kovalevsky, so that she might leave Russia in order to continue her studies. In 1869 Germany, she studied physics and math at the University of Heidelberg. The following year she was refused admission to a Berlin university due to being a woman, so she instead studied privately with a well-known mathematician.

In 1874, she was awarded a doctorate from the University of Gottingen for three papers. Marie Curie's paper on partial differential equations—which was thought to be the most impactful work—gave Curie significant recognition inside the European mathematical community. Kovalevskaya went on to gain a reputation as a writer (for her novels, plays, and essays), an advocate of women's rights, and a political activist.

Marie Curie's ascent in the world of scientific research was at a crucial turning point for women in history, where the scale was just beginning to tip in women's favor, and progress was finally possible. If Curie had been born even fifty years earlier, it is possible her incredible discoveries would have been lost.

THE BLACK EXPERIENCE IN FRANCE AT THE TURN OF THE CENTURY

Black French women had an even harder time than white women in turn-of-the-century France. Although on April 27, 1848, slavery was abolished in all French colonies by the provisional government, racism continued to affect the country's people. The racism in France was not like the racism in the United States at the time, which was severe: anti-black riots, lynchings, and segregation made life for most black people extremely hard to impossible. Racism in France was not part of the institution and systems in place, and so revealed a different world for black people than the United States offered.

However, black people in France in the late 1800s and early 1900s endured racist **caricatures** and campaigns depicting them as uncivilized savages. There were disgraceful "shows" where black people were walked

An unnamed black woman in early 1900s France, where black people had rights not given in the United States

through the streets in order for whites to view them. A black man called "Chocolate the black clown" was physically abused, and was often used as a symbol of **colonialism**. However, France also could mean a new freedom for a black person, especially for those coming from America.

\When World War I began, France desperately needed black citizens to join the war effort, and hundreds of thousands did, in fact, join. After being promised French citizenship, many thousands of black men died. At the end of the war, black people were kept from being a part of the peace negotiations. One hundred and seventy-one African Americans were awarded the French Legion of Honor.

During World War I, many black men introduced their French counterparts to jazz and blues music. The twenty-eight American black regiments in World War I were accompanied by bands and bandmasters.

The band of the 369th Infantry became famous, led by James Reese Europe, a musician whose syncopated style played alongside the dancing of Vernon and Irene Castle, creating a dancing craze. These army bands playing a new, instantly beloved music became popular in France. This popularity extended beyond the troops and to French civilians.

THE NOBEL PRIZE IS CREATED

Alfred Nobel was born in 1833, in Sweden, but spent his childhood in Russia. As an adult, he invented and obtained a patent for dynamite, after which he opened an explosives company and became incredibly wealthy, moving to a large home in the center of Paris. Nobel's invention of dynamite had unexpected consequences: the proliferation of violence through the use of dynamite in anarchist bombings.

A man of many interests, including literature, music, science, and philosophy, Nobel was inspired in part to leave his fortune for a greater good by Bertha Von Suttner. Von Suttner had been Nobel's assistant before leaving to take up the fight for peace, organizing the Austrian Peace Society and writing the antiwar novel, *Lay Down Your Arms*. Nobel and Von Suttner had become fast friends, and Von Suttner was the first woman to win a Nobel Peace Prize in 1905.

In Nobel's will, written on four short pages on November 27, 1895, in Paris, he specified that his fortune (the bulk of it left after allowances for those closest to him) be divided into five parts, and used for prizes in physics, chemistry, medicine, literature, and peace, given to "those who, during the preceding year, shall have conferred the greatest benefit to mankind."

When Nobel died the next year, this unprecedented will attracted attention throughout the world. Although many were pleased with the humanitarian effort, Nobel's relatives were not happy and contested

LITTLE CURIES

Marie Curie gave crucial aid to the war effort during World War I in the form of small ambulance services called "Little Curies." When the war broke out, Curie realized that the service of X-ray machines could be crucial in saving lives on the battlefield, but there was no way of bringing the heavy machines to the soldiers. Curie sought out her rich friends to lend Renault trucks, which she planned on modifying to use as portable X-ray machines.

Curie also convinced X-ray machine manufacturers to donate machines and electric generators, and she asked body shops to donate their services in outfitting the trucks with the equipment. Curie taught over 150 volunteers to take X-rays with the machines, and soon the Little Curies were on the field. Curie and her daughter Irène volunteered in the battlefields with the Red Cross.

When injured soldiers came into a field hospital, the hospital would contact Curie through the Red Cross. Curie, and often Irène as well, would drive to the hospital (Curie learned how to drive during the war) and set up their machines, taking X-rays of injured soldiers so that surgery could be performed if deemed necessary. By the end of World War I, Curie had examined over one million wounded soldiers.

Marie Curie poses alongside one of her Little Curies.

the will. Many also criticized the international scope of the prizes, protesting that they should be restricted to Swedes. Of course, not many years later, the Nobel Prize would become hugely significant to the Curie family, opening the doorway for worldwide recognition for the brilliance of Marie Curie, as well as providing important funds for Curie's research.

THE FIRST WORLD WAR

World War I began on July 28, 1914, and lasted until November 11, 1918. The war was centered in Europe, on the Franco-German borders, and infamously began with the assassination of Austrian Archduke Franz Ferdinand and his wife, Sophie, by a Serbian nationalist in Sarajevo on June 28, 1914. Subsequently, there was a standoff between Austria-Hungary, Serbia, and Russia, who supported Serbia. Germany declared war on Russia and a mere two days later, France. Immediately, France declared war against Germany, getting troops ready for the provinces of Alsace and Lorraine, which France had been given to Germany in the Franco-Prussian War settlement of 1871.

Eventually, the Great War—as it was known at the time—involved Germany, Austria-Hungary, and the **Ottoman Empire** (Central Powers) against Great Britain, France, Russia, Italy, and Japan (Allied Powers). In 1917, the United States joined the war as part of the Allied effort.

World War I was fought on land and sea and in the sky as well. Throughout the conflict, new and deadly technology brought terrible suffering and unprecedented death. In particular, World War I is known for "trench warfare," an extensive system of dug trenches from which men on both sides fought. Overall, this complicated and bloody war cost over thirty-eight million human beings their lives.

A newly married Marie Curie stands in the laboratory with Crookes tubes.

THE FIELD AND CULTURE OF SCIENCE IN THE 1800S AND 1900S

T he history of physics begins in scattershot time periods around the world, but all science began with the desire to understand the workings of the natural world that human beings perceived around them. The Mayans of Mexico and Central America were one of the first known civilizations to use scientific measurements such as a calendar, tracing the movements of the planets, moon, and sun, and using a place system for numbers, including the first use of zero.

PHYSICS EVOLVING OVER TIME

In Europe, the first civilization to utilize science was the Greeks, around 600 BCE. They had the early idea that the world was divided into invisible elements—a foreshadowing of atoms. The famous Greek, Aristotle, put forth four earthly elements, consisting of earth, water, air, and fire. Each element claimed its place by weight, so earth, the heaviest, was the center of this universe, while water was above earth, air above water, and then fire above all these.

Archimedes, a scientist-engineer and one of the most important geniuses of humankind, advanced scientific experimentation and thinking. Among his many accomplishments was to discover the principle of buoyancy of a body in liquid, and the calculation of an accurate value for pi.

After the fall of Rome in about 400 CE, Greek learning was lost to the Dark Ages in Europe but kept alive by its transmission and translation in the Middle East. Middle Eastern knowledge was added to Greek knowledge, resulting in important discoveries and mathematical breakthroughs. Over time, this ancient knowledge made its way to Europe again.

Francis Bacon, an Englishman born in London in the late 1500s, was the founding father of the scientific method as we know it today. He developed a scientific methodology that involved gathering data, analyzing it through experimentation, and documenting results in order to best gain knowledge. René Descartes, a Frenchman born in 1596, offered an important contribution to science: an analytic approach, breaking a problem down into orderly parts and arranging them logically, otherwise known as **reductionism.**

After this early knowledge, the scientific thinkers became more profuse, and advancements in thinking and method proliferated. Physics took a backseat to chemistry and mathematics until the 1800s, when English schoolmaster John Dalton took a renewed interest in the theory of atoms. Dalton proposed an atomic explanation of how ratios of whole numbers always combined precisely by mass in gases, offering that the gases were formed of atoms whose masses were also in the ratio of simple **integers.** In simpler terms, Dalton was providing a mathematical explanation for exactly how atoms were organized. Much later, in 1869, Dmitry Mendeleev in Russia constructed the first period table using Dalton's atomic description along with the knowledge that certain groups of elements had similar chemical properties.

It was at this point that physicists had begun to believe—wrongly— that they had discovered the most basic and crucial elements of their scientific focus. New breakthroughs were about to explode throughout the scientific world, of which Marie Curie would be a crucial element.

WILHELM CONRAD RÖNTGEN

To understand the history of human beings and radiation, we begin with Wilhelm Röntgen, born in 1845 in Germany. Despite the fact that he was not particularly gifted in his schoolwork, Röntgen became adept at building mechanical objects and spent much time outdoors, experimenting in nature.

After a circuitous route involving an expulsion at age sixteen, Röntgen was accepted as a student of mechanical engineering at Polytechnic at Zurich. This, finally, was a good fit, and Röntgen received his diploma as a mechanical engineer in 1868, as well as a doctorate of philosophy degree one year later. He was then accepted as the assistant to August Kundt, professor of physics, who would become an important mentor for Röntgen. It was in Zurich that Röntgen met Anna Bertha Ludwig, who he married in 1872.

The next handful of years were a series of professional accomplishments for Röntgen, including taking the position of chair of physics at the University of Giessen, and eventually becoming **rector**, or head, of the University of Würzburg, where he would accomplish his most important work.

In 1895, Röntgen was working in his laboratory in Würzburg, conducting experiments with a Crookes tube. Crookes tubes were named after William Crookes, who discovered that a tube coated in

Wilhelm Conrad Röntgen, the scientist who discovered the X-ray

fluorescent material at the positive end produced a concentrated "dot" when rays from an **electron** gun hit it. Cathode tubes, as they were originally called, function with two interior elements: On one side of the tube there is a cathode and an anode. The cathode is a negatively charged conductor while the anode is a positively charged conductor. Electrons, which are negatively charged, come from the cathode, drawn toward the anode. A minor hole in the anode permits a small amount of electrons to pass through, creating an electron beam. On the opposite side of the cathode tubing is a coating that illuminates when the electrons hit it.

Crookes tubes were shaped like a bulb, and Röntgen had been experimenting with the range of cathode rays, or the beams of electrons, outside the reach of those bulbs. He was passing an electric current through gases at low pressure and saw that rays were emitted during the passage of current through the discharge tube. Röntgen worked an experiment in a completely darkened room with a covered discharge tube, resulting in rays that illuminated a barium platinocyanide–covered screen, which in turn became fluorescent despite the fact that the cover was in the path of the rays, and was 9 feet (2.7 meters) away— too far away to be caused by the cathode rays. Röntgen determined that the lit screen had been caused by invisible rays originating from the Crookes tube and began a series of intensive, focused experiments around this hypothesis.

Continued experiments revealed that these rays were capable of passing through many substances but left bone and metal visible. Röntgen used a photographic plate to capture the image of different objects of various thicknesses, in the path of the rays. The first, now famous, X-ray was of Röntgen's wife Anna's hand, her wedding ring clearly visible, of which she exclaimed, "I have seen my death."

Röntgen continued his experiments over the next seven weeks, and immediately submitted a provisional paper, "On a New Kind of Rays," in the Proceedings of the Würzburg Physico-Medical Society. Following this, he lectured at the same society, and then demonstrated

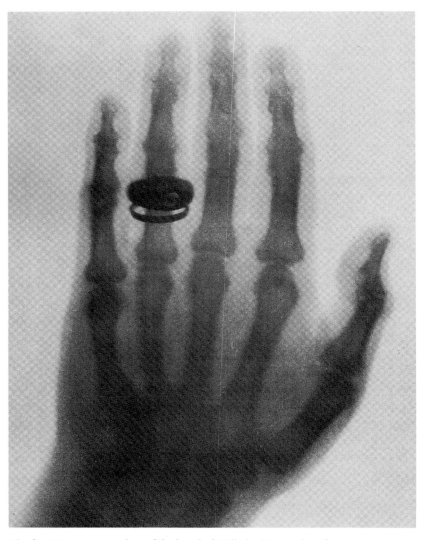

The first X-ray image taken of the hand of Wilhelm Röntgen's wife, Anna

the X-ray by making a plate of the hand of an attending **anatomist**. The anatomist proposed that the discovery be called "Röntgen's rays," although Röntgen himself simply called them X-rays.

This discovery was enormous, and Röntgen was immediately showered with honors and awards. As cathode tubes were commonly used in scientific experiments, scientists all over the world could immediately begin experimenting with Röntgen's findings. Like Marie Curie, Röntgen was a fervent believer in the importance and position of experimental data in science, asserting:

❝ *[T]he experiment is the most powerful and the most reliable lever enabling us to extract secrets from nature, and that the experiment must constitute the final judgment as to whether a hypothesis should be retained or be discarded.* **❞**

There was such scientific fervor over Röntgen's discovery of X-rays, and the desire to experiment in order to find the conditions under which X-rays could be best produced, that an Englishman named Sydney Rowland curated a journal devoted entirely to rounding up the new scientific data being accumulated. The journal was called *Archives of Clinical Skiagraphy* and was released later the same year as Röntgen's discovery.

Physicists and electricians were also speculating on X-rays: What was the essential nature of these rays? Thomas Edison even weighed in, suggesting that the rays might be acoustical or gravitational. Eventually, three distinct possibilities rose to the top, all electromagnetic in origin: the waves might be longitudinal, they might be high-frequency light, or they were **transverse** impulses of the ether.

HENRI BECQUEREL

Henri Becquerel was a French physicist who, at the time of Röntgen's discovery, was the physics chair at École Polytechnique. Becquerel had prowess with phosphorescent materials, uranium, and laboratory research, including photography, allowing him particular **acuity** in his

Henri Becquerel, the man who discovered radioactivity

research following the discovery of X-rays. Becquerel's experimentation revolved around the question of whether there was an elementary connection between radiation and visible light, so that any luminescent material would bring about X-rays.

In order to test his hypothesis, he exposed an arrangement of phosphorescent crystals upon a photographic plate—wrapped in opaque paper—to sunlight for several hours. After being developed, the photographic plate revealed silhouettes of the crystals. Further experimentation followed, and soon Becquerel reported his discovery to the Académie des Sciences in February of 1896, noting that certain salts of uranium were particularly active.

What brought the most notice to Becquerel at the time was the remarkable finding that stimulating the crystals with light was not necessary; that in fact, it appeared the uranium was emanating X-rays all by itself. With further experimentation, he found that even crystals kept in darkness retained penetrating radiation. At the time, Becquerel incorrectly supposed that this was the result of a long-lived phosphorescence. Becquerel had discovered something amazing that would change Marie Curie's life as well as all humankind: radioactivity.

CLASSICAL AND MODERN PHYSICS

In order to better understand the significance of not only Röntgen and Becquerel's discoveries but also Marie Curie's to come, it's crucial to appreciate where our understanding of physics was in the late 1800s. This period of time was involved in the study of "classical physics" and was teetering on the edge of the study of what we now call "modern physics."

Classical physics is defined as including the foundations for physics prior to the twentieth century: in general, including Newton's laws of mechanics, a theory of electricity and magnetism unified in Maxwell's equations, and **thermodynamics**. At the moment of Marie Curie's immersion into physics experimentation, the overall accepted working theory was not that matter is built out of atoms, but instead, that matter was continuous. In general, the scientific community believed they understood the fundamental principles of nature, and that the largest problems of physics had been solved. Looking beyond what can be seen with the naked eye and into the atomic structure of existence marked the beginning of modern physics.

The cultural attitude toward, and impact of, science itself had been waning in the later 1800s. There was a concern that science was merely bringing about a rise in harmful technology that created pollution and overcrowding, in addition to stripping away a spiritual foundation for the natural world as we know and perceive it to be. It was with Wilhelm Röntgen's discovery of X-rays and the creation of photographs that the cultural shift toward the value of science truly began.

At a rapid rate, Röntgen's discovery went from marvelous find to practical application. Within a month of announcing Röntgen's discovery, medical radiographs were built in Europe as well as the United States, to be immediately utilized by surgeons. Within six months, X-rays were being used on the battlefield to locate life-threatening bullets in wounded soldiers. This kind of societal impact dramatically changed the cultural view of the importance of science, but it was another man whose work in physics truly marked the end of the classical era in physics and the beginning of the modern era.

THE WORK OF MAX PLANCK

Karl Ernst Ludwig Max Planck was born in Kiel, Germany, on April 23, 1858. In 1867, after his family moved to Munich, Planck was taught by Hermann Muller, who awoke Planck's interest in physics. It was also in Munich that Planck obtained degrees from the Universities of Berlin and Munich, focusing on thermodynamics, or the study of heat and energy. Planck said of physics:

❝ *The outside world is something independent from man, something absolute, and the quest for the laws which apply to this absolute appeared to me as the most sublime scientific pursuit in life.* **❞**

During Planck's professorship of theoretical physics at the University of Berlin, he composed the entirely new idea of the quanta. Planck found that energy was not emitted in a steady continuum, but instead was delivered in distinct values: this finding is now called Planck's Constant. In 1900, he presented his quantum theory at the Physikalische Gesellschaft in Berlin. The theory was then published in the *Annalen der Physik*, and further summarized in two books. It is said that Planck's findings, although not realized for their extreme importance immediately, were the turning point between classical and modern physics.

Although not related to his scientific findings, it is equally important to note that Planck was a deeply moral man who made a powerful stand for human rights during the war, and who resigned his post as president of the Kaiser Wilhelm Institute in protest of Hitler's actions against Jewish scientists. After the war ended, the Kaiser Wilhelm was renamed the Max Planck Institute, with Planck himself appointed as its head.

LISE MEITNER'S FORGOTTEN LEGACY

Lise Meitner was born November 7, 1878, in Vienna, Austria, to a large, Jewish family. Like Marie Curie, Meitner had a father who insisted on the intensive educating of his daughters, despite prevailing mores of the time, which discouraged this. Lise was naturally talented in mathematics, and as girls were not permitted to attend the boys' high school, Meitner passed the difficult entrance exam to the University of Vienna. At twenty-three, she was the first woman admitted to the university's physics laboratories and lectures; she was the second woman to receive a PhD in physics from the university.

Physicist Max Planck traveled to Vienna during this time, and Meitner and Planck made each other's acquaintance. In 1907, Meitner said yes to Planck's invitation to do her postdoctoral research in Berlin, where she worked for several years as an unpaid research scientist. She was disallowed access to the laboratories of the Berlin Institute for Chemistry due to her gender and the risk that her hair could catch fire. It was this same year that Meitner and radiochemist Otto Hahn became research partners, discovering radioactive elements and engaging in what would become a rich collaboration stretching over thirty years.

Meitner's important research allowed her into a forward-moving group of physicists, including Albert Einstein, who would gather at Planck's home for conversation and collaboration. Like Curie, Meitner worked in primitive laboratory conditions, putting in long hours deep into the night. After being offered an assistant professorship elsewhere, she was finally given a paid position at the Berlin Institute for Chemistry in 1913. In 1918, she was appointed head of the physics department of the Kaiser Wilhelm Institute.

Meitner's career in physics was incredibly productive and successful, but the fact that she was a woman, and Jewish during World War I, directly disrupted and abbreviated her legacy. In 1923, she isolated the cause of the emission from atomic surfaces of electrons with signature energies. In 1925, French scientists independently came to the same finding and thereafter, the phenomenon was known as the "Auger effect."

Meitner and Hahn together discovered the first long-lived **isotope**, ore of the element protactinium. Meitner did much of the work herself as Otto was serving in World War I. In 1939, Meitner and fellow Austrian physicist Otto Robert Frisch published in the journal *Nature*, describing something incredible: the splitting of a uranium atom into two lighter elements of barium and krypton. They termed the process "fission." This was the beginning of the discovery of **nuclear fission**. However, Meitner never received proper credit for this important work.

Hahn and physicist Fritz Strassman confirmed the presences of krypton but did not give Meitner's role the credit due, and she was hardly mentioned in their published paper. Meitner wrote to Hahn, "[I]t would have been so nice for me if you had just written that we—independently of your wonderful findings—had come upon the necessity for the existence of the Kr-Rb-Sr series."

It is believed that due to fear of the Nazi regime, Hahn continued to minimize Meitner's role, and he alone was awarded the 1944 chemistry Nobel Prize for the discovery of fission. Meitner never received the physics Nobel Prize. Her later career was full of prizes, awards, accolades, and eventually, an element: meitnerium.

THE ROADBLOCKS FOR WOMEN IN SCIENCE IN THE EARLY TWENTIETH CENTURY

One of the most distressing aspects of the history of science is the elimination of the names of women who made significant contributions. Categorically, women have been entirely stripped of their accomplishments, and often their accomplishments were then later attributed to men. Lise Meitner and Marie Curie had in common that they had to, from the very beginning of their scientific interest, fight for every opportunity to learn, to practice, and to have their scientific findings published and accredited to them.

European universities didn't take women as students until the 1880s and 1890s, and black women had no avenues to pursue higher scientific education. Institutions providing higher education to women included slightly over three thousand women in 1875, and by 1900, female students numbered almost twenty thousand. Despite Marie Curie's fame and importance in the early 1900s, female scientists were considered little more than a "bride of science," always a mere attendant or assistant to the more important male scientists, who were considered to be doing the "real" and important theorizing and research. In addition, many men did not want female scientists working in their laboratories; for example, Max Planck did not work with female scientists before his meeting with Lise Meitner.

Possibly the largest barriers to women interested in pursuing science included family of origin and financial standing. Women like Marie Curie and Lise Meitner, who had a parent—specifically, a father, who wielded the most financial influence—supporting their education and advanced pursuits had a great advantage, perhaps a crucial one. Without the intervention of a father determined that his daughter receive a thorough education, a woman had little opportunity to do so herself.

Financial standing was also crucial, although as it occurred in the life of Marie Curie, it was possible for families of lesser means to accomplish the goal of a university education for their daughter, if this education was considered worthy enough a goal for hard work and sacrifice. Marie Curie was able to attend the Sorbonne due to her hard work as a nanny and tutor for years before moving to Paris, and her agreement with her sister in a trade-off of financial support, as well as the small amount of money her father was able to send during her university years. In addition to this, Curie was fortunate to fall in love with Pierre Curie, a scientist devoted to laboratory research who wanted to work alongside his talented wife. In fact, it has been noted that Pierre had been in a serious relationship with a woman only once before. This woman had died fifteen years before Pierre met Marie, and after his first love's death, Pierre had been unhappy to realize that none of the women he subsequently met were interested in science.

Other barriers to women in science during this time included the realities of marriage, childbirth, and parenting. A woman who worked as a scientist and married usually became pregnant at some point, and the combined rigors of scientific research as well as bearing a child are incredibly difficult. Of course, a woman was expected to sacrifice all career interests in order to be a mother, and Marie Curie was roundly and widely criticized for her continued focus on laboratory experimentation after the births of her daughters, Ève and Irène Curie.

Another female scientist who was actively working in the early 1900s was Ida Tacke. Like Marie Curie, Tacke discovered two new elements, rhenium and masurium. However, the discovery of masurium does not exist in the record books. That is because Tacke's male contemporaries felt that this element could not possibly naturally occur on the planet, despite Tacke's excellent evidence. It was not until two male scientists created the element in a lab that the element was given a place, and a new name, technitium. Those two male scientists were given full credit for the discovery of this element.

Tacke also worked from a theory that elements above uranium were in existence, and wrote a paper explaining that, when hit with massive amounts of **neutrons**, the particles could be broken down to reveal a ton of energy. Eventually, scientist Enrico Fermi was awarded the Nobel Prize for his discovery of the production of radioactive elements during neutron bombardment. Tacke died in 1978, unrecognized for her achievements.

After Irène's birth in 1897, Curie's father-in-law joined the household in order to assist in caring for the home and child. Curie originally left the laboratory to breastfeed, but after deciding this was too distracting, she hired a wet nurse. Her devotion to research and

Marie Curie was far from a traditional mother of her time, but she worked hard to ensure her daughters had all advantages. Here she poses with Irène.

exhausting laboratory hours was the source of later derision from the public at large.

Female scientists who were white, came from families that supported higher education for women, and who had the money to fund such an education still had many roadblocks in the world of science. For female graduates, there were few if any job opportunities, with teaching at a women's college being the main option.

Women in science were cosigned to "women's work," such as laboratory assistants to scientists or secretarial, note-keeping work for research scientists, and regardless of the actual work that a female scientist did, she was usually left out of all papers, conferences, and awards, and therefore, history.

ALBERT EINSTEIN'S AMAZING DISCOVERIES

Albert Einstein was born in Ulm, Germany, on March 14, 1879, and grew up in Munich, Germany. He famously didn't speak much until three years old, worrying his parents enough to have him brought to the doctor, but Einstein was simply on his own timeline. His father, an electrical engineer, owned an electronics company, so Einstein was able to learn about science and electronics at an early age. His father also gave him a compass when he was bedridden with an illness at five years old, sparking what would be a lifelong fascination with the invisible workings of the universe.

In 1894, Einstein's family moved from Munich to Pavia, Italy. This was the same year Einstein wrote his first scientific paper, "The Investigation of the State of Aether in Magnetic Fields." His education continued in Switzerland, and in 1896, he joined the Swiss Federal Polytechnic School in Zurich for teacher training in physics and mathematics. After graduation, Einstein could not find a teaching position, so he settled into a post as a patent officer at the Federal Office for Intellectual Property in Bern. It was here that he founded a science and philosophy group named the Olympia Academy.

Einstein's "miracle year" was the year of 1905, because this was when the completely unknown scientist, at twenty-six years old, published

THE VALUE OF SCIENCE

"For the admirable gift of himself, and for the magnificent service he renders humanity, what reward does our society offer the scientist? Have these servants of an idea the necessary means of work? Have they an assured existence, sheltered from care? The example of Pierre Curie, and of others, shows that they have none of these things; and that more often, before they can secure possible working conditions, they have to exhaust their youth and their powers in daily anxieties. Our society, in which reigns an eager desire for riches and luxury, does not understand the value of science."

—Marie Curie

four groundbreaking papers in the *Annalen Der Physik*, one of the best-known and regarded physics papers of the time. Einstein's first paper applied Max Planck's quantum theory of the quanta to light, explaining what is called the **photoelectric** effect, where a material will emit electrically charged particles when hit with light. Moving further into Einstein's genius, the next paper illustrated his analysis of Brownian motion, where he experimented with proving the existence of atoms. The last and third research, entitled "On the Electrodynamics of Moving Bodies," introduced Einstein's theory of relativity, while a fourth paper illuminated the relationship between mass and energy, revealing Einstein's famous $E=mc^2$ equation.

Einstein believed that his $E=mc^2$ equation might explain Marie Curie's discovery at the time, that just one ounce of radium emitted 4,000 calories of heat per hour indefinitely, apparently violating the laws of thermodynamics. He formulated the theory that as radium radiated energy, there would be a reduction in mass. "The idea is amusing and enticing; but whether the Almighty is laughing at it and is leading me up the garden path—that I cannot know," he wrote.

At first, these incredible papers were met with silence. However, then Max Planck, the important quantum theorist whose work had inspired one of Einstein's own theories, publicly lauded Einstein's findings, and it was then that the scientific world realized the astonishing breakthroughs that had been revealed.

After this incredible year, Einstein's life changed completely. He lectured at international meetings and was offered several high positions at important institutions, the last of which was the University of Berlin, which he accepted. He served as director of the Kaiser Wilhelm Institute for Physics from 1913 to 1933.

After the publications of his papers in 1905, Einstein became preoccupied with a hole in his own quantum theory: the lack of explanation for the action of gravity in terms of the curvature of space-time. It was in 1907 that Einstein found the crucial element missing, through a vision: a man falling off a roof. The man would be accelerating, falling—unlike a beam of light, which moves at constant velocity. And yet, Einstein realized, the falling man would also be at rest, exerted upon by the matter of the universe. This was Einstein's principle of equivalence, which held that gravitational acceleration was indistinguishable from acceleration caused by mechanical forces. Therefore, gravitational and inertial mass were identical. It wasn't until 1915 that Einstein solved the math to prove his theory.

Marie Curie and Albert Einstein slowly formed a friendship of deep, mutual respect.

In 1919, Einstein's life again changed forever. This was the year that Arthur Eddington, a famous astronomer, proved Einstein's theory of relativity. Einstein proposed that a solar eclipse on May 29, 1919, offered a rare chance to observe gravity's effect on light. Eddington decided to put the theory to the test. To prepare, he arranged two expeditions to observe the event. One expedition would observe in Brazil, and the other off the west coast of Africa. As the sky became dark and the stars appeared, if Einstein's theory was correct and the sun pulled on the passing light, the stars near the edge of the sun would appear to be out of position to the exact degree his equations predicted.

In September, Einstein received word that his predictions had been correct, and in October, he received acknowledgement from the most important physicists. This was expected. What happened next, however, was not. On November 7, the world woke to the *Times of London* headline, "Revolution in Science, New Theory of the Universe. Newtonian Ideas Overthrown." The public response was enormous. Einstein was officially famous, despite British astronomer Joseph Norman Lockyer announcing that Einstein's discoveries "do not personally concern ordinary human beings; only astronomers are affected."

Now it was not only physicists fascinated with Einstein's mind but the public at large. It is widely accepted that the explanation for the public's voracious appetite and appreciation for Einstein's work lies with the aftermath of World War I. Millions of people had been killed in one of the bloodiest and most traumatic wars ever fought. Countries around the world were terrorized, heartbroken, and searching for some comfort in the light of humankind's potential for devastation. During some of the darkest days of man's existence, Einstein had been painstakingly, doggedly, and joyfully theorizing and proving an entirely new construction to the building blocks of our universe. It is no surprise that his seemingly magical discoveries captured the imaginations of a wearied world.

A photo of Wladyslaw Sklodowski with his grown daughters; left to right: Marie, Bronya, and Hela, circa 1890

CHAPTER FOUR

THE CONTEMPORARIES AND STRUGGLES OF MARIE CURIE IN HER WORKING YEARS

Marie Curie was born into a family oppressed by the harsh Russian czar's rule over Poland and financially broken due to the consequences of their political beliefs. Still, she was lucky in particularly important ways: her father and mother were intellectuals and devoted parents, both of whom ensured academic rigor and advanced learning for all their children, male and female.

It is perhaps the true foundation of Marie Curie's lifelong devotion to scientific research that she was raised by parents who believed, to such a degree that they risked their lives, in revolution through ideas. The Sklodowskis felt that the Poland they loved so much would be freed through the development of the mind, and the willingness to devote one's life to hard work. Their close family bonds and obvious enjoyment of each other's company throughout their lives suggest that this was not a dour household full of grim and determined people, but instead a family imbued with purpose and meaning.

In addition, the Sklodowskis did not attribute this need for learning and work to only their son. Marie Curie and her sisters all received from their father the same language lessons, mathematical lessons, and poetry and literature readings as their brother, as well as the support of their family in achieving a higher education, something very rare for women of that time—especially women from families of little means. Surely watching her mother run a girl's school, while still lovingly raising her family and encouraging them all in intellectual pursuits, made a deep, lasting impression on Marie Curie: that a life well lived, for both man and woman, was one that included both family and constant learning.

Eventually, Curie's older sister, Bronya, set off to Paris to achieve her dream of becoming a medical doctor—she became director of the Radium Institute of Warsaw—and this too was an inspiration for young Marie Curie. Plans that were made for higher education were not merely dreams but could be achieved in actuality.

THE SORBONNE INFLUENCERS

Marie Curie's education at the Sorbonne University in Paris, France, was the definitive turning point in her life. There, she rose above her fellow students with her outstanding marks and academic achievements, and she was able to immerse herself in the intellectual world that had been beyond her reach beforehand. She wrote, "It was like a new world opened to me, the world of science, which I was at last permitted to know in all liberty."

She engaged with Paul Affel, the dean of the science department at the Sorbonne, who gave lectures. She was influenced by the important scientist and lecturer Professor Gabriel Lippmann, professor of experimental physics, and later director of the research laboratory. Professor Lippmann became a member of the Academy of Sciences in 1886, serving as president in 1912.

Professor Lippmann was an important supporter of Curie's early scientific focus and served as her thesis advisor. He allowed Curie to use his laboratory for her thesis work. Lippmann created the first color photographs and spent several years working out the complex physics of his theory. Professor Lippmann's theory was based on the interference phenomenon, which involves the merging of different light waves, and requires a coating of mercury behind the photographic plate's emulsion. His work earned Lippmann the Nobel Prize in 1908, but his system of color photography was never widely used due to the complex and expensive procedures necessary, and the inability to copy the final color photograph.

MEETING PIERRE CURIE

During Curie's hard work, a professor helped her receive a research grant to study the magnetic properties and chemical composition of steel. Curie was looking for crucial laboratory space when she was introduced to Pierre Curie, a brilliant scientific researcher himself. Pierre was Lab Chief for the Paris Municipal School of Industrial Physics and Chemistry, and at age thirty-five, ten years older than Curie. Pierre was deeply respected in the international scientific community, but in the actual workings of the French scientific community, he acted as somewhat of an outsider. He did not care about his career or receiving acknowledgment of his work, reflecting his upbringing. As a child, Pierre had not attended an elite French school but had been taught by his father, who was a physician, his mother, and, at age fourteen, by a private mathematics teacher. Pierre was both the son and grandson of physicians, and his father was an eager scientific enthusiast. As a boy, Pierre observed experiments performed by his father, igniting Pierre's passion for experimental research. At the early age of eighteen he had

Pierre and Marie Curie with their wedding gifts of new bikes, on their way to their honeymoon

already earned the equivalent of a higher degree, and he enrolled in the Faculty of Sciences during the time he was still a probationary pharmacy student. He received a license in physical sciences in November 1877. Pierre's only sibling, his brother Jacques, was a laboratory assistant to Charles Friedel at the Sorbonne mineralogy laboratory. Pierre and Jacques started a scientific collaboration in the physics of crystals.

When Pierre was eighteen, he and Jacques discovered the phenomenon of **piezoelectricity**, or the difference in electrical potential that is seen when mechanical stresses are applied on certain crystals, including quartz. In 1878, Pierre was appointed laboratory assistant to Paul Desains at the Sorbonne physics laboratory. In 1882, he became director of laboratory work at the École Supérieure de Physique et de Chimie, where he was to spend twenty-two years deep in research and experimentation. Jacques Curie was appointed professor of mineralogy in 1883, at the University of Montpellier. This ended the scientific collaboration of the two brothers.

Pierre spent much of his time in the laboratory inventing and perfecting measuring devices, which were to become a crucial element in the work he did with Curie on radioactivity. One of the most important inventions had been created with Pierre's brother Jacques; this was using piezoelectric quartz in an instrument for making absolute measurements of very low electrical currents. He built a **quadrant** electrometer, or an **electrometer** that used four separate parts to measure electricity, improving upon the one devised by Lord Kelvin by adding an clever magnetic damper. Marie used the Curie electrometer to measure the slight currents passing through air that has been filled with uranium rays. The electric charge could vanish with the moist air of the workroom, but Curie was able to gather reproducible measurements.

Working together, Pierre and Marie Curie fell in love, and after some time, Pierre proposed marriage. Curie had some difficulty deciding to accept or not, as marriage would mean she was permanently settling in Paris, and not Poland, where most of her family lived. Eventually she accepted, and they were married in a quiet ceremony in July 1895. There was no ring exchange, and famously, Curie wore a dark blue outfit instead of a wedding dress, so that she could reuse it as a lab garment in the years afterward.

Curie had no intentions to marry, as she knew her life would be devoted to science. In Pierre Curie, she found a perfect compliment: a man as absorbed with scientific discovery as she, and a man who was able to see and accept her as his equal. By all accounts, the Curies shared a respectful, productive, incredibly meaningful life together and remained deeply in love until Pierre's untimely death.

When the Curies had their first child, daughter Irène, in September 1987, immediately the problem of childcare was clear. As Curie said:

> **❝** *It became a serious problem how to take care of our little Irène and of our home without giving up my scientific work. Such a renunciation would have been very painful to me, and my husband would not even think of it ... So the close union of our family enabled me to meet my obligations.* **❞**

After her father-in-law, Dr. Curie, moved into the household, he was able to take over babysitting his granddaughter Irène, and the problem was solved. Irène and her grandfather had a very close bond for the rest of his life. Meanwhile, Pierre and Marie Curie settled in to their constant, steady laboratory work.

HENRI BECQUEREL'S IMPORTANT DISCOVERY

On November 8, 1895, Wilhelm Röntgen made his discovery of X-rays. In January 1896, he made his first public presentation on his discovery and sent out a collation of his findings to colleagues, including Pierre Curie. Pierre then addressed the Academy of Sciences on the discovery of these "Röntgen rays." Scientist Henri Becquerel was very interested in these rays and the connection between them to the phenomenon of fluorescence. He began experimenting and made his own discovery, that

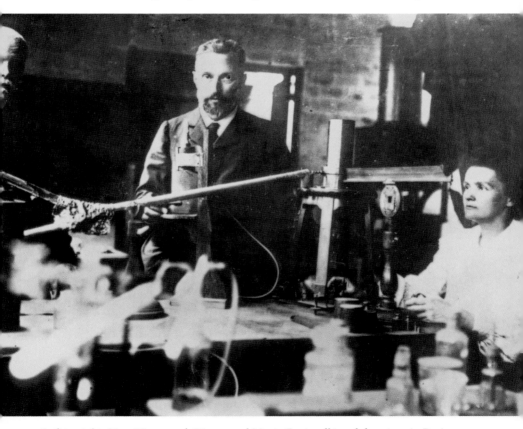

Left to right: *Henri Becquerel, Pierre, and Marie Curie, all in a laboratory in Paris, France*

which Marie Curie would later identify as radioactivity. At the time, a serious lack of interest was shown to Becquerel's findings. Instead, the scientific community was focused on Röntgen's discovery—that is, with the exception of Marie Curie.

In order to obtain her doctorate, Curie had to choose a subject. She settled on uranium radiation, inspired by Becquerel's work. She began to study uranium emissions using the machine developed by Pierre, and she soon confirmed that the amount of radiation coming from the uranium was proportional to the concentration of uranium. This was the beginning of the scientific discoveries that would change Marie and Pierre Curie's life—and humankind. Without the building block of Becquerel's findings, it is impossible to know what would have resulted from Curie's alternate doctorate work.

ALBERT EINSTEIN AND MARIE CURIE

Albert Einstein and Marie Curie had a mutual friend before they met each other, a physicist named Henrik Lorentz. Lorentz won a Nobel Prize in 1902 for the mathematical theory of the electron, proposing that light waves were caused by oscillations of an electric charge in the atom. This was before electrons had been proven to exist. Lorentz is also known for his work on the Fitzgerald-Lorentz contraction, which is crucial to Einstein's special theory of atoms as well as theories of relativity. This contraction includes transformations that describe the increase of mass, the reduction of length, and the time dilation of a body that is moving at speeds most like the velocity of light.

Lorentz was a friend of both the Curies and Einstein, so they would meet in 1909 at the First Solvay Conference in Brussels. This meeting began a powerful professional and personal relationship between Marie Curie and Albert Einstein, solidified by mutual respect. It was also in 1909 that Marie Curie assisted Einstein in obtaining a position as teacher for theoretical physics at the University of Zurich.

Einstein would visit Marie Curie, stay with her family, and take vacation with them as well. On one occasion, they vacationed in the Alpine passes of Switzerland. They hiked with Einstein's wife at the time, Mileva, and his daughters, who were of the same general age as Curie's daughters. Einstein stood up for Curie during a terrible scandal, famously writing to her:

> **"** *Highly esteemed Mrs. Curie, Do not laugh at me for writing you without having anything sensible to say. But I am so enraged by the base manner in which the public is presently daring to concern itself with you that I absolutely must give vent to this feeling. However, I am convinced that you consistently despise this rabble, whether it obsequiously lavishes respect on you or whether it attempts to satiate its lust for sensationalism! I am impelled to tell you how much I have come to admire your intellect, your drive, and your honesty, and that I consider myself lucky to have made your personal acquaintance in Brussels. Anyone who does not number among these reptiles is certainly happy, now as before, that we have such personages among us as you, and Langevin too, real people with whom one feels privileged to be in contact. If the rabble continues to occupy itself with you, then simply don't read that hogwash, but rather leave it to the reptile for whom it has been fabricated.*
>
> *With most amicable regards to you, Langevin, and Perrin, yours very truly,*
>
> *A. Einstein* **"**

Einstein and Curie also collaborated together in the International Committee on International Cooperation of the League of Nations, which she felt was imperfect but still held real hope for the future. Curie persuaded Einstein to join the group. After her death, Einstein spoke at the Curie Memorial Celebration and praised his friend for "her strength, her purity of will, her austerity toward herself, her objectivity, her incorruptible judgment—all of these were of the kind seldom found in a single individual."

MISSY MELONEY, THE US JOURNALIST AND SUPPORTER OF CURIE

Marie (Missy) Meloney was a United States journalist and magazine editor who held Marie Curie in the highest regard. Curie was notoriously private, refusing most press and interviews, including those journalists traveling to Paris who Meloney pressed to request an interview with Curie. Finally, Meloney herself sent Curie a note, "My father, who was a medical man, wrote: 'It is impossible to exaggerate the unimportance of people.' But you have been important to me for twenty years, and I want to see you for a few minutes." This approach worked. Curie agreed to an interview with Meloney in May 1920.

Weeks before, Meloney had visited Thomas Edison in his own surroundings and laboratory, and found him well off, as she believed such an important member of the scientific community should be. In contrast, she found Marie Curie in a very simple apartment, working in what she considered an inadequate laboratory. In reality, Curie was financially sound and did have her own laboratory, **rudimentary** as it was. Missy Meloney wrote about Marie Curie as if she were impoverished and created what history has looked back on as a hyperbolic version of the actual Marie Curie.

Meloney felt that the need for assistance must be stressed so that Curie could have her research wishes fulfilled; primarily, more radium with which to work. Even more specifically, 1 gram (0.035 ounces) of radium to begin with. Meloney promised Curie that fundraising would begin, and the radium would be obtained. Meloney returned to the United States, and over the course of the next year raised the $100,000 necessary to purchase the gram, and convinced Curie to come to America to receive the radium in an official ceremony.

Marie Curie arrived in New York City aboard the ship *Olympic* in 1921. Along with her were her two daughters, Irène, twenty-three years of age, and Ève, sixteen. This was the first transatlantic trip for Curie, who was in her fifties at this time. Crowds of supporters greeted them, as well as the cheerful music of a live band. On May 20, Curie was received at the White House by President Warren G. Harding, who personally handed over the radium to the French scientist. The rest of Curie's trip was a whirlwind of activity, with receptions and many visits to laboratories of universities and colleges that awarded her honorary doctorates. At each laboratory visit, Curie was talkative and inquired on the processes of the laboratory. She made a very pleasurable impression on the scientists, who were impressed with her knowledge and expertise, and who then often made donations of money or equipment. Six weeks later, Curie returned to France considerably financially emboldened, as well as having made strong connections with overseas scientists. Missy Meloney was to stay a good friend for the rest of Curie's life.

THE FRENCH ACADEMY OF SCIENCES

In the beginning of 1911, Curie announced her candidacy for chair in physics at the Academy of Sciences. The Academy was the most powerful scientific organization in France, where members read their scientific papers, held conventions, and endowed scientific grants. Curie had impeccable qualifications. In 1903, she co-won the Nobel Prize for Physics for her work in finding the radium element. Marie Curie's accomplishments were incredible; she headed the Sorbonne physics laboratory, earned a doctorate in science, and was the first female professor of general physics. Yet she was not born in France, and was commonly said to be a Jew during a time rife with **anti-Semitism**, even though she was not Jewish, and most of all, she was a woman. Even other women publicly disapproved of the idea—important writer Julia Daudet wrote that science was useless to women.

Curie found herself on the wrong end of an angry right-wing media, who brought up the fact that Curie was a Polish woman who had made antiwar statements. Her primary competition was engineer Edouard Branly. Branly discovered radioconduction, called the Branly effect. In 1890, he noted that an electromagnetic wave alters metal filings' ability to conduct electricity, and he used his discovery to make a very sensitive detector called a coherer. Advanced versions of the coherer became the first practical wireless signal receivers. Branly did have some against him in the Academy due to his avowed Catholic faith, but he also had great champions for that same reason. French patriots had also been angered when Italian Gugliemo Marconi was awarded the 1909 Nobel Prize for Physics instead of Branly.

French physicist Emile Hilaire Amagat said at the time, "Women cannot be part of the Institute of France." In January 1911, the Academy voted; President Armand Gautier announced that all could enter the chamber—except women. Marie Curie received twenty-eight votes, Eduard Branly thirty. After this, Marie Curie would not publish papers with the Academy for ten years, effectively cutting off her relationship with the larger scientific world. Although her papers were published in smaller, more specific magazines, the Academy was the only one read by the world's scientific community.

MARIE CURIE AND PAUL LANGEVIN

Pierre Curie died at the age of forty-six on April 19, 1906. At the time, he had already been ill, showing signs of severe radiation poisoning, such as tremors, great arthritic pain, and open sores. Marie Curie coined the term "radioactivity" for the very thing that would make both herself and her husband ill, and eventually kill her. In a paper by Pierre Curie and Becquerel, they detail some of the hazards of working with radiation:

❝ *After these effects we have described, we experimented on our hands the different actions during researches with these very active products. Hands have a general trend to become scaly, and the extremities of the fingers which held tubes or capsules containing very radioactive products become hard and sometimes very painful. For one of us, the inflammation of the extremities of the fingers lasted about 15 days and finished when the skin dropped off, but the painful sensation did not disappear for two months.* **❞**

Despite all the signs of poisoning, Pierre Curie did not die from radiation exposure; instead, he lost his footing in the Paris streets and was hit by a horse-drawn carriage. He died immediately. When Marie Curie was told of his death, she repeated over and over, "Pierre is dead. Pierre is dead." Pierre Curie had made clear his wishes in the case of his death: no special ceremony, no event, no great gathering. Instead, a family attended a private burial in a Sceaux family tomb. Marie Curie ensured that his wishes were met, and afterward, she

A harrowing painting depicts Pierre Curie's moment of death underneath a horse-drawn carriage.

refused the government's offer of a pension. She did, however, take up the offer of her husband's position as the Sorbonne, becoming the first female professor at the great university.

In 1910, Curie began an affair with a former student of Pierre's, Paul Langevin. Marie Curie described Langevin in a letter to a friend as owning a wonderful intelligence. Langevin had, in fact, discovered that $E=mc^2$ only to find that Einstein had just published a paper on the same discovery. Langevin was a mathematician and physicist, married to a woman with whom he had an unhappy and, at times, violent relationship. The friendship between Langevin and the widowed Curie turned into romance.

A drama began unspooling. Curie and Langevin began meeting covertly. Eventually, Langevin's wife found this out. Although she was aware of past infidelities on his part, this affair with the famous scientist Marie Curie (someone she had invited into her home as a friend) particularly enraged her. She threatened to kill Marie Curie, going so far as to accost Curie on the Parisian streets one night, threatening her life. Langevin assured Curie that his wife was, in his opinion, capable of such a thing, and so Curie momentarily fled to a friend's house.

Langevin and Curie agreed not to see each other, calming his wife, but during the International Congress of Radiology and Electricity— which both Langevin and Curie attended—Langevin's wife became convinced they were using the meeting as an opportunity to restoke their affair. She threatened to publicly expose them.

At Eastertime that same year, Langevin's wife hired a detective. The detective snuck into a hotel room that Curie and Langevin were sharing during a tryst and took love letters back to Langevin's wife. Soon afterward, the letters were published in Paris newspapers. The public went crazy with this information. People threw stones at the windows of Curie's home and called out names, so she took her daughters to a friend's house. The press printed letters that Curie had written Langevin, giving specific instructions on how to leave his wife, and called her a homewrecker, a Jew, and a Polish **temptress**. Many colleagues turned their backs on Curie during this time.

Paul Appel was a friend and colleague who thought that Curie should leave Paris and move back to Poland. He was going to demand that Curie do so, but his daughter, whose home Curie was staying at, told him that were he to do so, she'd never talk to him again. In response, he threw a shoe at her, but he ultimately did not speak to Curie about moving.

LORD KELVIN

As Curie focused on her work, she was publicly called out in the *Times* of London by Lord Kelvin, a scientist. Lord Kelvin, or William Thomson, is considered one of the world's great physicists. The term "applied science" has been given to the type of work that he created.

Lord Kelvin formulated the dissipation of energy principle, in the second law of thermodynamics. His engineering made it possible to lay the first telegraph cable across the Atlantic Ocean. He invented a mariner's compass, a temperature scale, instruments for receiving cable signals, and a deep-sea sounding **apparatus**. He wrote voluminous articles and lectures.

He publicly declared that Curie's radium was instead helium. His motivation was a disagreement in an important theory: the age of the earth. Lord Kelvin had placed the earth at 20 to 50 million years old, while Curie had used her research in radioactivity and the life of its elements to claim an Earth age of twice Lord Kelvin's estimation. Curie spent three years working with pure radium and discerning its atomic weight in order to prove her theory correct.

Although Paul Langevin was the one actually married, no one threw stones at his house or demanded that he leave the country. Langevin did, however, challenge journalist Gustave Tery to a **duel** after Tery wrote insults about Langevin. Duels were illegal at the time, but frequently held. The journalist accepted, so they met on the street with pistols in hand. In the end, neither would shoot.

Marie Curie suffered tremendously, both personally and professionally. She won a second Nobel Prize in Chemistry, and shortly after being notified of her prize, she was written a letter from the Nobel Committee requesting that she refrain from traveling to Sweden and claiming it. She wrote back, in part: "In fact the Prize has been awarded for the discovery of Radium and Polonium. I believe that there is no connection between my scientific work and the facts of private life … I cannot accept the idea in principle that the appreciation of the value of scientific work should be influenced by libel and slander concerning private life. I am convinced that this opinion is shared by many people."

Curie attended the Nobel Prize ceremony with daughter Irène, and no one spoke of personal matters. Afterward, Curie fell into both mental and physical illness. She lost a great amount of weight and wrote of contemplating suicide. Her kidney was diseased as well, and she had an operation on it in February of that year. Around this time, family friends cared for Irène and Ève, and they were not to see their mother for almost a year.

OPPOSITION TO MARIE CURIE

Although Marie Curie kept her focus on her scientific work, in simply existing as a female scientist, she was shaking up long-held beliefs and structures about women and workplace, women and science, and women and higher ranking organizations and positions. Inevitably, she encountered serious opposition during her lifetime. It was only after a member of the nominating committee, a professor of mathematics named Gösta Mittage-Leffler, who was familiar with Marie's leading role in the Curies' work, wrote to Pierre, that a conspiracy to exclude her from the 1903 Nobel Prize in Physics was overcome. Pierre Curie wrote to the Academy himself: "If it is true that one is seriously thinking about me for the Nobel Prize, I very much wish to be considered together with Madam Curie with respect to our research on radioactive bodies." So it was that one-half of the prize was awarded to Becquerel for his discovery, the other half to Pierre and Marie for their joint work on the radiation phenomena discovered by Becquerel.

France had reached the peak of growing **sexism**, **xenophobia**, and anti-Semitism that defined the years preceding World War I. When Curie's nomination to the French Academy of Sciences was rejected, there were many accusations flung at her. Perhaps the most ridiculous accusation was that this Nobel Prize–winning scientist, Marie Curie, was merely riding the coattails of her deceased husband, Pierre. First-wave feminism was active in Paris. Marie Curie was in the public eye during a time when political lines were being harshly drawn in private and public over the stand a person took on women's rights.

French feminism started as the seed of desire to replace Catholic monarchy with a republican government. Feminists, emphasizing reformation in family law and economic legalities, built organizations, published journals, and congregated with powerful people around the world, yet the movement stayed divided. First-wave feminists were set apart from the general public of French women because of questions pertaining to how a woman could have rights, yet still retain her crucial role in the family. There was debate and internal conflict over a woman's right to work, and how advocating for that right might put motherhood and the family as an entity at risk. Anti-feminists were able to convince the general public that feminism would create **amoralism** and disintegration of the French society. Marie Curie's affair with Paul Langevin gave opportunity for all these biases to come to a head. Her work and her accomplishments, as well as her lack of mothering, had clearly turned her into a homewrecker. In addition, some claimed, she wasn't even truly French, but Polish, and probably Jewish. Every volatile prejudice and fear of the time was directed toward Marie Curie, both publicly and privately. It is no wonder she suffered an intense physical and mental breakdown as a result.

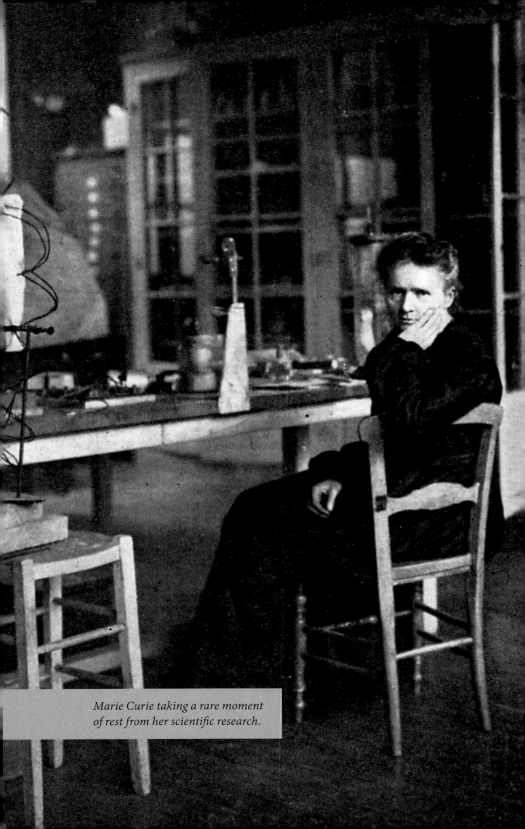

Marie Curie taking a rare moment of rest from her scientific research.

CHAPTER FIVE

THE SCIENTIFIC ACCOMPLISHMENTS OF MARIE CURIE

Once Marie Curie began her doctoral work at the Sorbonne, all her natural gifts and years of intensive studying and experimenting culminated in the beginning of one of the most important scientific discoveries of all time.

As a child, Curie was noted to have a **prodigious** memory. She began reading at the precocious age of four. Later, during her years as a nanny in Poland, she self-taught as well as attended lessons at the Floating University. At the Sorbonne, Curie was able to focus on mathematics and physics, truly immersing herself in a new, broadening scientific world. She finished first in her master's degree physics course in 1893 and second in math the next year. Next she was commissioned through the Society for the Encouragement of National Industry to do a study comparing magnetic properties of various steels to their chemical makeup. This led her to search for a laboratory, which in turn led her to meeting Pierre. He assisted her in finding her laboratory space. In the summer of 1897, Curie submitted the results of her research to the Society for the Encouragement of National and received a payment.

She gave a lump sum of money to the scholarship fund from which she had received money four years earlier. This was not a requirement, but she desired to assist in the education of another bright Polish student.

CURIE'S THESIS STATEMENT BEGINS

Curie's thesis topic was the result of a perfect storm of scientists, ideas, and opportunity. It was in 1895 that Wilhelm Röntgen had discovered a kind of ray that could travel through objects and photograph people's bones. Röntgen's rays, or X-rays as he called them, became the darlings of the scientific world. Mere months after the discovery of Röntgen's rays, French physicist Henri Becquerel reported his research to the French Academy of Sciences. He found that uranium **compounds**, even completely kept in the dark, emitted rays that would fog a photographic plate. Although this research was noted, it was overlooked due to the intense focus on X-rays in the scientific community.

This was the perfect opportunity for Marie Curie, who needed a thesis that could be immediately researched without having to take in a long catalog of published papers. Because these findings were new, she could dive right in. She began laboratory experimentation in a storeroom at the Paris Municipal School of Industrial Physics and Chemistry, where Pierre was professor of physics. With the acute concentration and complete dedication to difficult, repetitive experimentation that she would become known for, Curie utilized a new device to perform her research. Years earlier, Pierre and older brother Jacques had invented an entirely new type of electrometer, a device for measuring extremely low electrical currents. Curie used the electrometer to measure the imperceptible currents that can pass through air that has been deluged with uranium rays. The storeroom air was damp, and this worked to dissipate the electric charge, yet she produced reproducible measurements. At the core of this work was the atom. At the time, scientists thought the atom was the most elementary particle, meaning there was nothing smaller, nothing contained in the atom itself. While the electron was discovered, nothing else was understood about the interior of the atom. Curie's work would challenge that notion, ultimately disproving it.

Because neither Marie nor Pierre were members of the Academy of Sciences, the report, "Rays emitted by uranium and thorium compounds," was presented April 12, 1898, by Professor Lippmann, Curie's professor at the time. Two conclusions were presented. The first was that the activity Curie had so precisely measured with Pierre's electrometers was an atomic property, not molecular, for two reasons. One, because the uranium activity was not dependent on the chemical state of the uranium, so the uranium had the same strength of activity, regardless of what chemical state it was in. Two, because the level of activity was always directly proportional to the amount of uranium in the compound being tested; in other words, the activity of the uranium could be predicted based on exactly how much uranium was present. Conclusion two proposed that an unknown element could be discovered by proving its radioactivity was different from that of any other known element.

Pitchblende is a uranium ore, a complex mineral composed of up to thirty various elements in combination. The Curies used a new method of chemical analysis to isolate the tiny amounts of unknown substances. They utilized various chemical procedures to separate the different substances in pitchblende. After separating materials into different compounds, radiation measurements were used to trace small amounts of unknown, radioactive elements among resulting fractions. They then used the electrometer to single out the most radioactive

Marie and Pierre sit with their daughter Irène on a Parisian bench.

Marie Curie: Radioactivity Pioneer and the First Woman to Win a Nobel Prize

fractions. This led to their discovery, which they named polonium, a way of honoring Poland, where Marie was born.

It was the Curies' next paper, "On a New, Strongly Radioactive Substance Contained in Pitchblende"—again presented to the Academy by Professor Lippmann—that gathered significant attention. They had found a new radioactive substance containing a new element: radium. It was after the presentation of this second paper that Curie was awarded a financial prize from the Academy of Sciences. The letters written to inform and commend Marie Curie on this prize were sent to her husband, with wishes to "pass on" their congratulations to Marie Curie.

THE ROMANCE OF SCIENTIFIC EFFORT AND THE COMPLETED THESIS

If there is a legend of Marie Curie, it was during this time that it was shaped. The grueling work of isolating polonium and radium from the bismuth and barium in which they were mixed began. The Municipal School storeroom was not suitable for this research so the Curies moved their lab to an abandoned shed across the school courtyard. This poorly ventilated shed was formerly a medical school dissecting room. Marie Curie wrote of this time in her book, *Autographical Notes*:

❝ *The School of Physics could give us no suitable premises, but for lack of anything better, the Director permitted us to use an abandoned shed which had been in service as a dissecting room of the School of Medicine. Its glass roof did not afford complete shelter against rain, the heat was suffocating in summer, and the bitter cold of winter was only a little lessened by the iron stove, except in its immediate vicinity. There was no question of obtaining* *the needed proper apparatus in common use by chemists. We simply had some old pinewood tables with furnaces and gas burners. We had to use the adjoining yard for those of our chemical operations that involved producing irritating gases; even then the gas often filled our shed. With this equipment, we entered on our exhausting work.* **"**

Marie Curie did the actual separation of the radium from the barium, while Pierre calculated the measurements following each step. It was tremendous physical labor to separate the radium from the barium; she had to work hard and laboriously with large vats of pitchblende. It was during this time that both Pierre and Marie began to show signs of radium illness, suffering from fatigue, burns, and weakness in their limbs.

The Curies received enormous amounts of pitchblende as a donation from the Austrian government. They collaborated with the company that marketed Pierre's scientific inventions, the Central Chemical Products Company. It paid for staff and product. Their colleague André-Louis Debierne assisted enormously by making the standard lab techniques fit with huge industrial order scales, meaning that the work could be used in a much broader market. The Central Chemical Products Company would eventually make a large profit by marketing the radium salts they received in return for their assistance.

Finally, their work paid off. After thousands of **crystallizations**, Curie isolated one decigram of almost pure radium chloride, determining radium's atomic weight as 225. She presented her doctoral thesis on June 25, 1903. The committee made it clear that the Curies' discoveries were the most significant scientific discoveries ever brought forth in a doctoral thesis, claiming it "très honorable." Curie's thesis was widely reprinted, including an English edition. It is also interesting to note that Marie and Pierre had made the decision to publish their data on radium, rather than obtain a patent. This meant that they received no profit from the data, although many companies did. These are Marie Curie's words on her thesis:

❝ *The object of the present work is the publication of researches which I have been carrying on for more than four years on radioactive bodies. I began these researches by a study of the phosphorescence of uranium, discovered by M. Becquerel. The results to which I was led by this work promised to afford so interesting a field that M. Curie put aside the work on which he was engaged, and joined me, our object being the extraction of the new radioactive substances and the further study of their properties.*

From the chemical point of view, one point is definitely established—i.e., the existence of a new element, strongly radioactive, viz., radium. The preparation of the pure chloride of radium and the determination of the atomic weight of radium form the chief part of my own work. **❞**

ERNEST RUTHERFORD'S EXPANSION OF MARIE CURIE'S FINDINGS ON ATOMS

Ernest Rutherford attended a dinner party held for Marie Curie after she was awarded her doctorate. (Which happened to have been thrown by no other than Paul Langevin, who would factor so prominently in Marie Curie's scandal after Pierre's death.) A brilliant physicist working in Canada with his associate Frederick Soddy, he came all the way to Paris to meet Marie Curie. He had begun to develop a hypothesis to explain the process of **radioactive decay**, or the change of an atomic nucleus into a lighter nucleus. Rutherford suggested that radioactive elements actually transform themselves, spontaneously breaking apart into the nuclei of other elements with smaller atomic masses. As this occurs, they emit radiation from their nuclei in one or more of the three forms. The spontaneous decay process endures until a stable nucleus is formed.

In order to understand what happens when radioactive atoms emit radiation, isotopes have to be understood. All atoms of the same element have the same number of protons in their nuclei. This means they have the same atomic number. However, atoms can have different numbers of neutrons even with the same element, and therefore different atomic masses. Isotopes from an element represent forms of that element, owning unique atomic masses. All isotopes of elements have identical chemical properties. As a radioactive nucleus emits alpha or beta particles, it changes into an atom of another element. The nucleus that undergoes decay is called the parent, and the nucleus into which it is transformed is called the daughter. Daughter nuclei can be unstable, as is the case with thorium. Marie Curie's radium and polonium are also radioactive decay products, daughters of uranium.

Rutherford and Soddy concluded this: each radioactive isotope owns one specific half-life. In other words, in a radioactive isotope half the nuclei decay in a defined period of time. The half-life of uranium 238 is 4.5 billion years, meaning during this timespan, half the nuclei in a sampling of uranium 238 will decay. For a contrasting example, polonium isotope, polonium 210, has a half-life that only spans 138 days.

An abbreviated half-life explains why the rigorous Marie Curie still could not isolate polonium.

Eventually, both Soddy and Rutherford (who is considered the father of nuclear physics) were awarded Nobel Prizes in Chemistry: Soddy in 1921 "for his contributions to our knowledge of the chemistry of radioactive substances, and his investigations into the origin and nature of isotopes" and Rutherford in 1908, "for his investigations into the disintegration of the elements, and the chemistry of radioactive substances."

FROM THE NOBEL PRIZE TO A NEW POSITION

At the end of 1903, the Royal Society of London presented Marie and Pierre Curie with the prestigious Davy Medal—named for the English chemist Humphrey Davy (1778–1829), who had also discovered several chemical elements. The following month, the Curies were awarded the Nobel Prize for Physics for their discoveries in radiation. Becquerel shared in the prize. It was found not many years ago that originally, the Nobel committee intended on awarding the prize to Becquerel and Pierre alone, excluding Marie Curie. Once Pierre was informed of this by a colleague on the board, he wrote to request his wife's inclusion. As Marie Curie had been in fact nominated the year before, she was included through renomination, and so the prize did go to all three physicists.

Although the Curies still did not have a suitable laboratory, with the Nobel Prize money, they were able to hire and pay a lab assistant. And perhaps more importantly, Pierre was finally offered a position as chair of physics at the Sorbonne. Originally, the offer did not come with a laboratory (as was custom), and Pierre turned it down. The Sorbonne immediately responded by finding the funds for the laboratory, along with three assistants. The senior chief of laboratory position was offered to Marie Curie. Finally, Curie would have a salary based on her important work.

Over the last few years, Pierre in particular had grown fragile and ill from the dangerous work he and his wife were undertaking. Although neither attributed their various ailments to radiation, this was clearly the cause. In July 1905, after the birth of their second daughter, Ève, Pierre's second attempt at election to the French Academy of Sciences was successful. This elected position did not seem to cheer Pierre, who was able to work but very little due to exhaustion, and who had not published any papers in recent years.

It was just over a year afterward, on April 19, 1906, that Pierre Curie was killed while crossing a rainy street in Paris. He was hit by a horse-drawn carriage, his head crushed, and instantly killed. The Sorbonne extended an unprecedented offer: would Marie Curie like to be the first female professor to ever teach at the Sorbonne? Marie Curie, after hesitating, decided to accept her late husband's position.

MARIE CURIE'S NEXT SCIENTIFIC STEPS AND ANOTHER NOBEL

It was at this time that Lord Kelvin issued a public challenge to Marie Curie with his letter to the *Times* stating that radium wasn't an element, but more likely a compound of lead and five helium atoms. This was more than just a friendly, professional disagreement. Lord Kelvin's theory threatened to ruin not only the Curies' entire scientific career, but also their colleague Rutherford's work in explaining the phenomenon of radioactivity. Curie responded by setting up and undertaking the

A SECOND NOBEL PRIZE

On November 7 a telegram was delivered to Marie Curie, informing her that she was receiving a second Nobel Prize, this time in chemistry. She attended the award ceremony on December 10, 1911. The president of the Royal Swedish Academy of Sciences spoke about why Marie Curie's 1898 discovery of two new elements deserved singular attention; he observed that this important work had greatly advanced scientific understanding of the nature of the atom itself, in addition to bringing forth never before known medical knowledge. The Nobel committee felt that the discovery of polonium and radium were so significant to chemistry that it had been very important not to lump in their discovery with the later discovery of radioactivity. Curie's scientific accomplishments were breathtaking in the implications for the future of science.

Not only had Marie Curie now won the Nobel Prize in chemistry, but she had become—and remains to this day—not just the first woman, but the first person to win a Nobel in two different categories. She won the second Nobel Prize in her name alone. Curie's impact on the scientific world was so important and revered that in 2011, the International Year of Chemistry, it was a stated goal to celebrate the centenary of her prize.

laboratory work necessary to prove that radium did own its spot in the periodic table. With the help of André Debierne, an old colleague of both hers and Pierre, she succeeded in 1910 in isolating pure radium metal. In order to achieve this, she had to separate radium from its salts, even though radium was only stable as long as it was chemically combined in a salt. Lord Kelvin died in 1907, before he was proven wrong.

In 1907, Marie Curie turned her concentration toward building up a fine laboratory in Pierre's memory. The American **magnate** and philanthropist Andrew Carnegie sent Curie's colleague Dean Paul Appel $50,000 to found the Curie Scholarships. Curie then assembled a laboratory research staff. In 1909, the Pasteur Institute (founded by the famous scientist Louis Pasteur) and the University of Paris began to collaborate on the founding of a Radium Institute. The Pasteur Institute hoped to advance research on radium's medical applications. The Radium Institute would include two divisions—a radioactivity laboratory that Curie would head, and a medical research laboratory.

"LITTLE CURIES" DURING WORLD WAR I

World War I began August 4, 1914. All male scientists, assistants, and scholars at the newly constructed Radium Institute were off to war. After the Germans bombed Paris in September, the French government was moved from Paris to Bordeaux, and many Parisians left along with it. Curie had sent her children and their housekeeper to stay in Brittany, while she herself transported the only supply of radium of France out of the state. At the government's request, she packed the single gram in a 45-pound (20-kilogram) lead box and took the train to Bordeaux, where she deposited the radium in a bank safe-deposit box.

Looking for a way to contribute to the war effort, she naturally turned to what she knew best: radiation. X-rays could save soldiers' lives

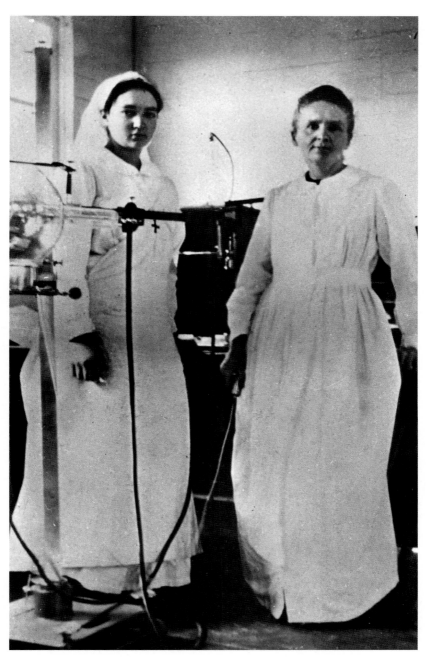

Irène (left) *and Marie Curie* (right) *working for the Red Cross during World War I.*

DR. ZHUANG XIAOYING: FOLLOWING IN MARIE CURIE'S FOOTSTEPS

Dr. Zhuang Xioaying (left) participates in an award ceremony in Berlin, Germany, in November 2015.

Dr. Zhuang Xiaoying was born in China in 1983 and studied from 2001 to 2007 at Tongji University in Shanghai. After Tongji University, she worked on her doctoral studies at the University of Durham, United Kingdom, completing her PhD in 2010. Dr. Xiaoying spent time as a postdoc in Norway, after which she returned to Tongji University in early 2011, first as a lecturer and then from 2013 to 2014, as an associate professor. Among many honors Zhuang has received are the Zienkiewicz Prize for the best PhD thesis in Computational Mechanics, and an EU Marie Curie International Incoming Fellowship, which enabled her to conduct research at Bauhaus University Weimar.

Dr. Xiaoying is focused on working with polymer-matrix composites (PMCs), man-made substances made of phases of construction, bound together in a sheet or fiber-wound form, which are broadly used in many scientific fields, yet their tolerance for damage, behavior, and performance have not been rigorously studied. She intends to design, optimize, and verify new materials using computer experiments and simulations. She is focused on the use of nanomaterials, or a material that is handled on an atomic or molecular level, in order to assist in the best use of PMCs for industrial purposes.

by helping doctors see internal damage. Curie used her considerable influence to get the government to agree to assist her in building the first military radiology centers in France. Curie was named director of the Red Cross radiology service. Most available X-ray machines were located in research laboratories rather than hospitals, so Curie used her influence within the scientific community to arrange for all of the available X-ray machines in French laboratories to be moved to various hospitals. By the end of the war, she had helped set up two hundred permanent X-ray stations throughout France.

Curie was further worried about the soldiers on the battlefields. She knew it was not always possible to transport wounded men to a hospital before operating, and she thought that if X-ray machines could somehow be more mobile, this could be a great service.

Curie was taught the use of X-rays for diagnostic purposes by Dr. Antoine Bècleré. Curie left immediately after to help treat wounded soldiers on the battlefield. She addressed her wealthy friends and requested donations of vans and funds. Curie then used her immense powers of scientific creativity and developed the first transportable X-ray machine. The "Petite Curies" (Little Curies) were ordinary cars that had been outfitted with X-ray equipment and a generator. The car's engine powered the generator, which then powered the X-ray machine. At first, the French Army would not allow for the machines, as the technology was so unique they did not believe it would truly be of help. It was not until military doctors on the front lines agitated for the lifesaving Little Curies that military leaders agreed to use the X-ray mobiles.

Curie and her daughter, Irène, took these machines to the battle front in the autumn of 1914 and ran the machinery themselves, working as "on call" units for the Red Cross. She established twenty mobile and

Marie Curie observes a cathode tube in the laboratory, one of her most basic and repeated modes of research.

two hundred stationary X-ray units. In 1916, she began to train women as radiological assistants at the Radium Institute. Curie also turned her considerable intellect toward creating a military radiotherapy service. She retrieved the gram of radium from its shelter in Bordeaux and began to use a technique to collect **radon**, a radioactive gas that radium emits on a consistent basis. Curie used an electric pump that collected radon in intervals of forty-eight hours, and next sealed the radon into glass tubes 0.4 inches (1 centimeter) long. The glass tubes were then transported to hospitals. At the hospitals, doctors covered the tubes in platinum needles, placing them precisely and directly within the patients, to destroy diseased tissue.

After the war, Curie wrote a book that summarized her experiences during the Great War, entitled *Radiology in War*. She continued working at the Radium Institute studying radium therapy until her death from aplastic anemia at age sixty-seven, on July 4, 1934.

MARIE CURIE'S WORK TODAY

Marie Curie's radioactivity led to new therapeutic and diagnostic methods in medicine. After Marie and Pierre Curie's papers were published, the applications of radioactivity began to be explored almost immediately. The Kassabian's Medical Manual was published in 1907 in Philadelphia (United States). The Kassibian manual itemizes tumors treated by radiotherapy—tumors that are still sometimes treated this way today.

Modern oncology is built on radiotherapy. The Radium Institute founded by Marie Curie eventually was joined by the Institut Curie, which today is a leading European cancer research group. The Institut has groups of biologists, chemists, physicists, **bioinformatics** specialists, and physicians. Honoring the legacy of their founder, Institut Curie

Irène and Frederic Joliot-Curie met and fell in love while working in Marie Curie's laboratory.

also hosts hospital students and interns, representing sixty nationalities. The Institut's goal is to spread medical and scientific innovations and knowledge throughout France and the world.

Radiotherapy led to **brachytherapy**, or radiotherapy where the radioactive source is in direct contact with the tumor tissues. Radium was first used in brachytherapy, placed directly on the body or in the vaginal canal or uterus of a woman. Around 1910, doctors began introducing the radiation **interstitially**, or deep into the tumor. This method was very dangerous for doctors applying the radiation until radioactive isotopes began to be used. Cancers of the head and neck are treated with brachytherapy, as are cancers of the genitourinary tract, and carcinoma of the penis. It can be used in replacement of disfiguring surgery, or also as a means to provide pain relief in cases of incurable cancer. Nuclear medicine is based on the discoveries of Marie Curie, where substances with radioisotopes are placed inside the organ of an ill person, in order to get a clear image of the tumor. It was Irène Joliot-Curie and her husband Frederic who advanced the progress of this treatment, with their scientific discovery of artificially created radioactive atoms.

IN HER MOTHER'S FOOTSTEPS: SCIENTIST IRÈNE JOLIOT-CURE

While her sister Ève became a writer who wrote, among other books, a biography of her mother, Irène always had scientific leanings. Her grandfather Eugene, to whom she was very close, taught her sciences from home. Her mother took over this teaching after Eugene's death, ultimately creating a collective school which emphasized mathematics, physics, and chemistry.

Joliot-Curie completed her doctorate after the war was finished. She worked at the Radium Institute in Paris and received a doctor of science degree for researching the radiation emitted by polonium, the element discovered and named by her parents. Joliot-Curie married Frederic Joliot, a physicist who worked with Marie Curie. Together, they began laboratory research on the composition of the atom, specializing in nuclear physics, or the science of the nucleus of the atom.

Between 1932 and 1934, the Joliot-Curies jointly published many important papers on the effect of alpha particles on various elements.

Twice, they closely missed important scientific discoveries that were made at the same time by other scientists. In the first instance, they wrongly interpreted the results of their measurements and missed that they had proven the existence of the neutron. Instead, it was James Chadwick who claimed the discovery of the neutron in 1932. In another experiment, the Joliot-Curies drew an incorrect conclusion about a mysterious outcome of their work, so shortly afterward, it was C.D. Anderson who claimed the discovery of the positron.

Finally, in January 1934, they conducted the nuclear transformation reactions in which they discovered artificial radioactive elements. It was at the Radium Institute that they found by bombarding stable elements with nuclear projectiles, they could create **artificial radioactivity**, or when a normal element is changed to a radioactive one through human interference. They first proved this with nitrogen, and afterward with aluminum and magnesium. About their achievements, Irène said:

> **❝** *We have shown that it is possible to create a radioactivity characterized by the emission of positive or negative electrons in boron and magnesium by bombardment with alpha rays.* **❞**

The Joliot-Curies were given the Nobel Prize in Chemistry in 1935 for their discovery. Irène Curie then became the second female scientist to win a Nobel Prize, after her mother. The Joliot-Curie discovery added hundreds of new radioisotopes to the period table. These new isotopes were then available for further scientific discoveries, such as how to release energy from an atom, as well as medicinal uses, such as further advancement in cancer treatments. In addition, the isotopes were relatively inexpensive, so they could be broadly used.

The Sorbonne played a formative role in Marie Curie's educational career.

Marie Curie: Radioactivity Pioneer and the First Woman to Win a Nobel Prize

After winning the Nobel, Irène Joliot-Curie was named a professor in the Faculty of Science in Paris. She researched nuclear fission, which is the splitting of an atomic nucleus. At the end of the 1930s, Irène became the under-secretary of state in terms of scientific research in the French government. In 1937, she was given the chair of the General Physics and Radioactivity in Sorbonne University. Joliot-Curie published over thirty scientific papers, most co-authored with Frederic. In 1946, she wrote a monograph on radioactivity.

Frederic Joliot-Curie, along with partners Hans von Halban and Lew Kowarski, had a marvelous discovery: new evidence that neutrons were put forth in the fission of uranium-235. This finding led to the probable reality of a self-sustaining chain reaction. Enrico Fermi and colleagues recognized the world-altering possibilities with this reaction—only if they could discover how to control it. On December 2, 1942, they did just that, creating the world's first nuclear reactor, dubbed a "pile." The pile consisted of uranium and graphite blocks, unbelievably (it seems today) built on the campus of the University of Chicago. This was the top-secret Manhattan Project, founded not long after the United States joined World War II. This secret project was to go on and develop the atomic bomb. The nuclear power industry was brought forth at the war's end, by expanding reactor types for large-scale power generation.

In 1947, Joliot-Curie was appointed the director of the Institute of Radium at the University of Paris and Commissioner for Atomic Energy. She assisted in the creation of the first French nuclear experiments. Like her mother, Joliot-Curie was denied membership to the Academy of Sciences. Eventually, she died at the age of fifty-nine of leukemia. Her husband Frederic would die two short years later, due to what he called the occupational disease.

Ultimately, Marie Curie left behind not only a wealth of scientific breakthroughs, but a family line of important physicists that continues. Irène Joliot-Curie's daughter and son both went on to become scientists; her daughter Helene became a professor of nuclear physics at the Institute of Nuclear Physics at the University of Paris, and director of Research at the French National Centre for Scientific Research. The Curie legacy lives on. About life, no one said it better than Marie Curie herself:

CC *Life is not easy for any of us. But what of that? We must have perseverance and above all confidence in ourselves. We must believe that we are gifted for something and that this thing must be attained.* **JJ**

CHRONOLOGY

1867   November 7, Marie Sklodowska is born in Warsaw (Poland).

1878   Marie Sklodowska's mother dies of tuberculosis.

1880   Pierre Curie and his scientific colleague and brother, Jacques, discover quartz piezoelectroscope.

1883   Marie Sklodowska graduates high school in Poland.

1889   The Eiffel Tower is complete; the First World Fair opens in Paris.

1891   Marie Sklodowska moves to Paris as a student of mathematics and physics at the Sorbonne.

1893   Marie Sklodowska graduates first place with a master's degree in physics.

1894   Marie Sklodowska is introduced to Pierre Curie; she earns her degree in mathematics.

1895   Marie Sklodowska and Pierre Curie are married on July 26; the Nobel Prize is established.

1896   Henri Becquerel discovers spontaneous radioactivity.

1897   Irène, the Curies' first daughter, is born; Curie begins her thesis work on Becquerel's uranium rays; Pierre abandons his work to join his wife's research.

1898	Marie and Pierre Curie publish hypothesis on existence of polonium; Marie and Pierre Curie publish discovery of radium.
1900	Marie Curie is appointed professor in the Superior Normal School for Young Women; Pierre is promoted to professor of the sciences at the Sorbonne.
1902	Marie Curie isolates radium and calculates its atomic mass as 225; Curie's father dies after a gallbladder operation.
1903	Curie defends her thesis, "Research on Radioactive Substances;" Marie and Pierre are awarded the Nobel Prize in Physics for the discovery of radioactivity, which they share with Henri Becquerel.
1904	The Curie's second daughter, Ève, is born on December 6; Pierre Curie is appointed the chair of physics at the Sorbonne; Marie Curie is appointed chief of laboratory in the laboratory of the chair.
1905	The Curies make a delayed trip to Stockholm to lecture on their discovery of radiation which won them the Nobel Prize; Einstein announces the special theory of relativity.
1906	Pierre Curie dies in a street accident at age forty-seven; Marie Curie replaces her husband as the professor of physics at the Sorbonne; Marie Curie assists in establishing a children's collective where daughter Irène and other children are taught privately.

1907	Marie Curie is awarded a large grant for scientific research from Andrew Carnegie.
1910	Curie isolates pure radium; Curie publishes "A Treatise on Radioactivity;" Curie begins affair with physicist Paul Langevin.
1911	Curie wins the Nobel Prize in Chemistry for the discovery of the elements polonium and radium, and for the isolation of radium; Curie is rejected for a seat at the Academy of Sciences.
1912	Curie has mental and physical breakdown; Curie has kidney operation.
1914	The Institute of Radium is built; Marie Curie named director of physics and chemistry laboratories; World War I begins.
1915	Marie and Irène Curie work on the battlefields delivering X-rays with Curie's invention "the Little Curies;" Einstein announces the general theory of relativity.
1918	Armistice signed between France and Germany, ending World War I.
1921	Marie Curie and her daughters visit the United States to receive 1 gram (0.035 oz) of radium from President Warren G. Harding and $100,000 for research.
1922	Curie is appointed to the Academy of Medicine.

1925	Irène Curie obtains her doctorate in science.
1926	Irène Curie marries fellow scientist Frederic Joliot.
1929	Curie visits the United States a second time to receive $50,000 for research as well as one gram of radium, and donates to Radium Institute in Warsaw.
1934	Curie dies of anemia on July 4 at the age of sixty-seven.
1935	Curie's daughter, Irène, and her husband Frederic Joliot receive the Nobel Prize in Chemistry for the discovery of artificial radioactivity.
1937	Ève Curie publishes a biography of her mother, titled *Madame Curie*.
1939	World War II begins.
1995	Pierre and Marie's ashes are transferred to the Pantheon.
2011	The Royal Society of Chemists celebrates a centenary since Marie Curie's Nobel Prize win.

GLOSSARY

acuity Sharpness; acuteness; keenness.

alloys A substance composed of two or more metals, or of a metal or metals with a nonmetal, intimately mixed, as by fusion or electrodeposition.

amoralism Not involving questions of right or wrong; without moral quality; neither moral nor immoral.

anarchy A state of disorder due to absence or nonrecognition of authority.

anatomist A specialist in anatomy: a person who analyzes all the part or elements of something with particular care.

anti-Semitism Discrimination against or prejudice or hostility toward Jews.

apparatus A group of machines or tools having a particular function or intended for a specific use.

artificial radioactivity The radioactivity of isotopes that have been artificially produced through the bombardment of naturally occurring isotopes by subatomic particles or by high levels of X-rays or gamma rays. Also called induced radioactivity.

baccalaureate A bachelors degree.

bioinformatics The retrieval and analysis of biochemical and biological data using mathematics and computer science, as in the study of genomes.

brachytherapy A form of radiotherapy in which sealed sources of radioactive material are inserted temporarily into body cavities or directly into tumors.

caricatures A picture, description, etc., ludicrously exaggerating the peculiarities or defects of persons or things.

clandestinely Characterized by, done in, or executed with secrecy or concealment, especially for purposes of subversion or deception; private or surreptitiously.

colonialism The control or governing influence of a nation over a dependent country, territory, or people.

compounds Composed of two or more parts, elements, or ingredients.

crystallizations A crystalized body or formation.

duel A prearranged combat between two persons, fought with deadly weapons according to an accepted code of procedure, especially to settle a private quarrel.

electrometer A calibrated device used for measuring extremely low voltages.

electron Also called megatron. An elementary particle.

emulsion Any colloidal suspension of a liquid in another liquid.

epistemological Pertaining to epistemology, a branch of philosophy that investigates the origin, nature, methods, and limits of human knowledge.

ideology The body of doctrine, myth, belief, etc., that guides an individual, social movement, institution, class, or large group.

integers Mathematics: one of the positive or negative numbers one, two, three, etc., or zero.

interstitially Anatomy: situated between the cells of a structure or a part, like interstitial tissue.

isotopes Any of two or more forms of a chemical element, having the same number of protons in the nucleus, or the same atomic number, but having different numbers of neutrons in the nucleus, or different atomic weights. There are 275 isotopes of the 81 stable elements, in addition to over 800 radioactive isotopes, and every element has known isotopic forms. Isotopes of a single element possess almost identical properties.

magnate A person of great influence, importance, or standing in a particular enterprise, field of business, etc.

metaphysical Pertaining to or of the nature of metaphysics. Philosophy concerned with abstract thought.

mores Folkways of central importance accepted without question and embodying the fundamental moral views of a group.

neutron An elementary particle having no charge, mass slightly greater than that of a proton, and a spin of half: a constituent of the nuclei of all atoms except those of hydrogen.

nuclear fission The main process generating nuclear energy. Radioactive decay of both fission products and transuranic elements formed in a reactor yield heat even after fission has ceased.

Ottoman Empire The Ottoman Empire, also known as the Turkish empire, Ottoman Turkey or Turkey, was an empire founded in 1299 by Oghuz Turks.

photoelectric Pertaining to the electronic or other electric effects produced by light.

piezoelectricity Electricity produced by the piezoelectric effect.

pitchblende A massive variety of uraninite, occurring in black pitchlike masses: a major ore of uranium and radium.

prodigious Extraordinary in size, amount, extent, degree, force, etc.

quadrant Something shaped like a quarter of a circle, as a part of a machine.

radioactive decay Radioactive decay, also known as nuclear decay or radioactivity, is the process by which the nucleus of an unstable atom loses energy by emitting radiation, including alpha particles, beta particles, gamma rays, and conversion electrons. A material that spontaneously emits such radiation is considered radioactive.

radon A chemically inert, radioactive gaseous element produced by the decay of radium: emissions produced by outgassing of rock, brick, etc. are a health hazard.

rector The head of certain Universities, colleges and schools.

reductionism The practice of simplifying a complex idea, issue, condition, or the like, especially to the point of minimizing, obscuring, or distorting it.

rudimentary Undeveloped, vestigial.

sexism Attitudes or behavior based on traditional stereotypes of gender roles.

suffrage The right to vote, especially in a political election.

temptress A woman who tempts, entices, or allures.

thermodynamics The science concerned with the relations between heat and mechanical energy or work, and the conversion of one into the other: modern thermodynamics deals with the properties of systems for the description of which temperature is a necessary coordinate.

transverse Lying or extending across or in a cross direction; cross.

typhus An acute infectious disease caused by several species of Rickettsia transmitted by lice and fleas and characterized by acute prostration, headache, and a peculiar eruption of reddish spots on the body.

xenophobia An unreasonable fear or hatred of foreigners or strangers or of that which is foreign or strange.

FURTHER INFORMATION

BOOKS

Conkling, Winifred. *Radioactive! How Irene Curie and Lise Meitner Revolutionized Science and Changed the World.* New York: Workman Publishing, 2016.

Curie, Ève. *Madame Curie.* New York: Da Capo Press, 2001.

Pasachoff, Naomi E. *Marie Curie and the Science of Radioactivity.* New York: Oxford Publishing, 1996.

Swaby, Rachel. *Headstrong: 52 Women Who Changed Science—And the World.* New York: Broadway Books, 2015.

WEBSITES

Embassy of the United States, Paris, France
http://france.usembassy.gov/whm2.html
A very helpful and short timeline of women's rights in France since 1790.

Fifteen Women Who Have Won Science Nobel Prizes Since Marie Curie
http://mentalfloss.com/article/53186/15-women-who-have-won-science-nobel-prizes-marie-curie
Meet these amazing female scientists who follow closely in the footsteps of Marie Curie.

Institut Curie

http://www.institut-curie.org

This website shows Marie Curie's work from over one hundred years ago, still going strong and saving lives.

Marie Curie Museum

http://en.muzeum-msc.pl/museum

The Polish Marie Curie museum.

Modern American Poetry

http://www.english.illinois.edu/maps/poets/m_r/rich/mariecurie.htm

A user-friendly, quick read that includes a sweep of the most important highlights of the life of Marie Curie.

The New Atlantis

http://www.thenewatlantis.com/publications/the-marvelous-marie-curie

A wonderful write-up on Marie Curie that contains interesting details about her life, specifically her childhood and young womanhood.

Radioactive

http://exhibitions.nypl.org/radioactive

This is an interactive website inspired by Marie Curie.

VIDEOS

Marie Curie: Great Minds

http://www.youtube.com/watch?v=r4jCTiGSuwU

This video features a young man telling Marie Curie's story with interesting puppets.

Radioactivity: Henri Becquerel, Marie, and Pierre Curie

http://www.youtube.com/watch?v=azwesgfZ1b8

A fifteen-minute video that begins with Röntgen's discovery of "a new kind of radiation" and works through Marie Curie's wonderful discoveries. Charming reenactments are incorporated along with a voiceover.

Women Who Changed the World: In the Footsteps of Marie Curie

http://www.youtube.com/watch?v=3HH_4D1V2rE

This video brings to life the accomplishments and history of Marie Curie.

BIBLIOGRAPHY

Calaprice, Alice, and Trevor Lipscombe. *Albert Einstein: A Biography*. Westport, CT: Greenwood Press, 2005.

Chiu, M.H., and P.J. Gilmer and Treagust, ed. *Celebrating The 100th Anniversary of Madame Marie Sklodowska Curie's Nobel Prize In Chemistry*. Rotterdam, The Netherlands: Sense Publishers, 2011.

Chodos, Alan, and Jennifer Ouilette, ed. "November 2, 1895: Roentgen's Discovery of X-rays." *APS News*. Ridge, NY. Vol. 10. Number 10. Accessed April 8, 2016. http://www.aps.org/publications/apsnews/200111/history.cfm.

Davies, Norman. "Revolution and Reaction." In *God's Playground: A History of Poland: Volume II: 1795 to the Present*. 272-279. Oxford University Press, 2005.

Davis, Amanda. "How Marie Curie Helped Save a Million Soldiers During World War 1." *the institute*, IEEE, February (2016) http://www.theinstitute.ieee.org/technologyfocus/technology-history/how-marie-curie-helped-save-a-million-soldiers-during-world-war-i.

Encyclopedia.com. "Curie, Pierre." *Complete Dictionary of Scientific Biography*, 2008. http://www.encyclopedia.com/doc/1G2-2830901043.html.

————. "Röntgen (Roentgen), Wilhelm Conrad." *Complete Dictionary of Scientific Biography*, 2008 http://www.encyclopedia.com/topic/Wilhelm_Conrad_Roentgen.aspx.

Emling, Shelly. *Marie Curie and Her Daughters: The Private Lives of Science's First Family*. New York, NY: Palgrave Macmillan, 2012.

Ermolaeva, Elena, and Jessica Ross. *Unintended Consequences of Human Actions*. University Press of America, 2010. Accessed April 22, 2016. Google Books.

Famous Scientists. "Albert Einstein." *Famouscientists.org*, July (2014) http://www.famousscientists.org/albert-einstein.

Fayyazuddin, Ansar. "Einstein's 1905 Revolution: New Physics, New Century." *SOLIDARITY*. May-June (2005): ATC 116. Accessed April 20, 2016. http://www.solidarity-us.org/node/58.

Ferry, Georgina. "Women In Science." *Encyclopedia Britannica*. Last Updated 2015. http://www.britannica.com/topic/Women-in-Science-1725191.

Froman, Nanny. "Marie and Pierre Curie and the Discovery Of Polonium and Radium." *Nobel Prize Organization* Translated by Nancy Marshall-Lunden. 1996. http://www.nobelprize.org/nobel_prizes/themes/physics/curie/index.html.

Glasser, Otto. *William Conrad Roentgen and the Early History of the Roentgen Rays*. Jeremy Norman Co; 2 Ed edition, 1992. Accessed May 3, 2016.

Goldsmith, Barbara. *Obsessive Genius: The Inner World of Marie Curie*. New York: W.W. Norton & Company, 2005.

Grolier Online. "Women's Suffrage." *SCHOLASTIC,* (2016) Accessed
April 15, 2016. http://www.teacher.scholastic.com/activities/
suffrage/history.htm.

Ham, Denise. "Marie Sklodowska Curie: The Woman Who Opened
The Nuclear Age." *21st Century Science and Technology,*
Winter (2002–2003) 30–68. Accessed April 15, 2016. http://
www.21stcenturysciencetech.com/articles/wint02-03/Marie_
Curie.pdf.

Jones, Elizabeth-Burton. "African American Exodus To Paris."
Georgetown Education Blog, Summer (2013) http://www.blogs.
commons.georgetown.edu/cctp-903-summer2013/2013/12/12/
african-american-exodus-to-paris.

Kamble, Dr. V. B. "Antoine-Henri Becquerel Discovery of
Radioactivity." *Vigyan Prasar Science Portal* U.P., India. Last
edited 2016. Accessed April 22, 2016. http://www.vigyanprasar.
gov.in/scientists/antoinehenribecquerel.htm.

Keene, Jennifer D. "French and American Racial Stereotypes During
The First World War." In *The United States and the First World
War.* Edited by Clive Emsley & Gordon Martel. Atlanta, GA,
2001.

Kulakowski, Andrzej. "The Contribution of Marie Sklodowska-
Curie to the development of modern oncology." *Analytical and
Bioanalytical Chemistry* 400 (2011): 1583-1586 Accessed April
15, 2016. DOI: 10.1007/s00216-011-4712-1. http://www.ncbi.nlm.
nih.gov/pmc/articles/PMC3093546.

La Berge, Ann Elizabeth Fowler, and Mordechai Feingold, ed. *French Medical Culture in the Nineteenth Century.* "Bacteriological Research and Medical Practice in and out of the Pastorian School" by Ann Marie Moulin. 327–343. Atlanta, GA, 1994. Accessed April 10, 2016. Google Books.

Lefferts, Peter M. "Black US Army Bands and Their Bandmasters in World War 1." *Digital Commons at University of Nebraska-Lincoln.* (2012) Accessed April 16, 2016. http://www.digitalcommons.unl. edu/cgi/viewcontent.cgi?article=1026&context=musicfacpub.

Masci, David. "Darwin and His Theory of Evolution." *Pew Research Center.* (2009) Accessed April 25, 2016. http://www.pewforum. org/2009/02/04/darwin-and-his-theory-of-evolution.

Mastin, Luke. "Max Planck (1858-1947)" *Physics of the Universe.* (2009) http://www.physicsoftheuniverse.com/scientists_planck.html.

Miller, Arthur. Prolouge to *Frontiers of Physics: 1900-1911: Selected Essays* (Studies; 15) Birkhouser, Boston, Inc, 1986.

Mirion Technologies. *Marie Curie, Henri Becquerel, Wilhelm Röntgen.* San Ramon, CA. http://www.mirion.com/introduction-to-radiation-safety/the-history-of-radiation.

Mould, R.F. "Pierre Curie, 1859-1906." *Current Oncology,* 14 (2007): 74–82. Accessed April 20, 2016. http://www.ncbi.nlm.nih.gov/pmc/articles/PMC1891197.

New World Encyclopedia contributors. "Marie Curie." *New World Encyclopedia* Accessed May 6, 2016. http://www.newworldencyclopedia.org/p/index.php?title=Marie_Curie&oldid=971339.

———. "Paris, France." *New World Encyclopedia* Accessed
April 9, 2016. http://www.newworldencylopedia.org/p/index.
php?title=Paris,_France&oldid=987026.

Pasachoff, Naomi. *Marie Curie And the Science of Radioactivity.*
New York: Oxford University Press, 1996.

Pycador, Stanley W. "Marie Sklodowska Curie and Albert Einstein:
A Professional and Personal Relationship." *The Polish Review,*
Vol 44, No. 2 (1999): 131–142. Accessed April 28, 2016. http://
www.jstor.org/stable/25779116?seq=1#page_scan_tab_contents.

Quinn, Sarah. *Marie Curie: A Life.* Cambridge, Massachusetts:
Da Capo Press, 1996.

Rayner-Canham, Marelene F and Geoffrey W. Rayner-Canham.
A Devotion to Their Science: Pioneer Women pf Radioactivity.
Philadelphia, PA: Chemical Heritage Foundation, 1997.

Rockwell, Sara. "The Life and Legacy of Marie Curie." *Yale Journal
of Biology and Medicine,* 76. (2004): 167–180. Accessed April 13,
2016. http://www.ncbi.nlm.nih.gov/pmc/articles/PMC2582731/
pdf/yjbm00205-0023.pdf.

Simanek, Donald E. "What's Classical Physics All About?" *A Brief
Course in Classical Mechanics.* http://www.lhup.edu/~dsimanek/
ideas/allabout.htm.

Zborowski, Krzysztof K. "Marie Sklodowska-Curie, A Brilliant
Child And A Talented Teacher." *arbor,* CLXXXVII, (2011), doi:
10.3989 Accessed May 2, 2016. http://arbor.revistas.csic.es/index.
php/arbor/article/viewFile/1247/1252.

INDEX

ABOUT THE AUTHOR

Maggie May Ethridge is a former educator now working as a full-time writer. A lifelong obsession with Marie Curie—beginning in elementary school with an oversized, illustrated children's book on the singular scientist's life—led her to the gratifying work of writing this short biography. In addition to her ongoing writing (including many published pieces of journalism, essays, short stories, and poems), Ethridge's memoir was published in 2015, and she recently completed a novel. She is enthralled with research, literature, culture, her family, and travel.

DATE DUE